THE BEGINNINGS
OF A LIFE OF PRAYER

THE BEGINNINGS
OF A LIFE OF PRAYER

Bishop Irenei
(M. C. Steenberg)

Second Edition

ST. HERMAN OF ALASKA BROTHERHOOD

2017

Address all correspondence to:
St. Herman of Alaska Brotherhood
P. O. Box 70, Platina, California 96076

www.sainthermanmonastery.com

Front cover: St. Anne's Skete, Mount Athos. Photograph by Stathis Haritopoulos, from *Agion Oros: Oi Agioi Topoi tis Makedonias* (Mount Athos: The Holy Places of Macedonia) (Thessaloniki: Ekdosis Efstathios Haritopoulos, 1997). Used with permission.

Back cover: Bishop Irenei blessing the faithful after the Divine Liturgy during which he was consecrated to the holy episcopacy. Cathedral of the Most Holy Mother of God "Joy of All Who Sorrow," San Francisco, November 6, 2016. Photograph by Sergei Kuzmin.

First Edition, 2012 (under the author's name Archimandrite Irenei)
Second Edition, 2017
Printed in the United States of America.

Publishers Cataloging-in-Publication

Steenberg, M. C. (Matthew Craig), 1978–
　The beginnings of a life of prayer / Bishop Irenei (M. C. Steenberg). —
2nd ed. — Platina, Calif. : St. Herman of Alaska Brotherhood, 2017.
　　p. ; cm.
　ISBN: 978-1-887904-29-2
　Includes bibliographical references and index.
　　1. Prayer—Eastern Orthodox Church. 2. Spiritual life—Orthodox Eastern Church. 3. Christian life—Orthodox Eastern authors. 4. Spiritual warfare. 5. Demonology—Orthodox Eastern Church. I. Title.
BX382 .S74 2012　　　　　　　　　　　　　　　　2012947657
248.4/819—dc23　　　　　　　　　　　　　　　　　　1210

CONTENTS

Introduction 7

PART I: TAKING STOCK OF OUR STRUGGLE 11
  The Call of Christ toward Self-Examination 13
  Attending to Our Struggles 22
  The Transformative Power of the Attentive Heart 55

PART II: THE BEGINNINGS OF A LIFE OF PRAYER 57
  The Beginnings of Prayer 59
  A Note on the Centuries on Prayer 72
  A Century on Prayer and Watchfulness 73
  A Second Century on Prayer: On the Preparation of the
    Mind and Heart 95

A Postscript: Prayer and the Cross 121

Scriptural Index 126

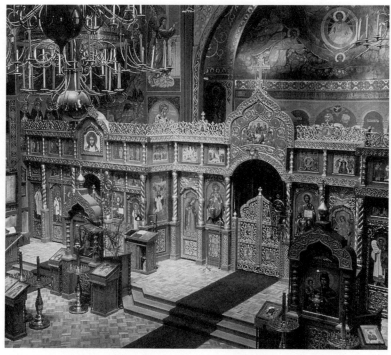

The Cathedral of the Most Holy Mother of God "Joy of All Who Sorrow,"
San Francisco, California. Photograph from *Joy of All Who Sorrow*
(San Francisco: Cathedral Editions, 2002).

INTRODUCTION

IT IS WITH some trepidation that I see this volume produced and published, given that it is on a topic—prayer—of which I cannot consider myself anything but a beginner. Yet for some years I have been asked to assemble a number of the talks, letters, and conversations on prayer that I have held in various contexts, and make them more widely available. The Fathers at St. Herman's Monastery in Platina, California have labored with great patience and love to make this book available, for which they have my deep gratitude.

The majority of what is printed here has its source in conversations and correspondence I have had over the past ten or twelve years, which I have endeavored to excerpt from letters, papers, and recordings and revise into cohesive form. Most of these conversations have been with monks and nuns, and so will reflect something of that context; but I hope that what is expressed—which is essentially a sustained reflection on the Church's teaching about prayer, through the testimony of her Fathers—might be of some small value to all those seeking to live the Christian life.

Two portions of this volume have been previously published in *The Orthodox Word:* namely, *Taking Stock of Our Struggle* and *A Century on Prayer and Watchfulness.*[1] In both cases, the versions provided in *The Orthodox Word* have been revised, updated, and expanded as part of the larger volume.

---

[1] The former as "Taking Stock of Our Struggle" in *The Orthodox Word,* no. 263 (2008); and the latter as "A Century on Prayer" in *The Orthodox Word,* no. 268 (2009).

To write a book on prayer is, at its heart, a paradoxical endeavor. We write down words about that which, in its purest form, is wordless; we pen phrases that are heard by the intellect, about an act that strives to go beyond the intellect. Yet, as a loving and holy spiritual elder once told me, "We must all make a beginning, and though crutches may eventually be cast away, for a time they are necessary to help us stand." At best, the reflections to follow are just that: crutches for beginners, offered solely in the hope that perhaps, somewhere among them, might be found a word here or there that offers some support to those beginning to pray.

May the Lord reward His servants who seek to follow Him with all their heart!

Archimandrite Irenei[2]
March 12/25, 2012
Sunday of St. John of the Ladder

Additional Notes for the Second Edition

It was with some surprise that I was informed by the Fathers of St. Herman's that the first edition of *The Beginnings of a Life of Prayer* had sold out and the need had arisen for a second printing. It is humbling to think that so many have found this little book of some use—and it is my hope that it has been precisely that: something of use in the actual life of prayer, rather than a collection of thoughts or reflections that merely pique the curiosity of the mind.

In the four years that have passed since the original printing, the world has tasted bitter turmoil and various upheavals in social, political, and moral realms. The days have often seemed

---

[2] In 2016 Archimandrite Irenei was consecrated and enthroned as Bishop of Sacramento (Russian Orthodox Church Outside of Russia).

dark. Injustice has sometimes seemed to gain the upper hand. Despair and fear have become bywords of a world of increased bitterness and division.

But to those ailing with spiritual illnesses in every age, the Church always prescribes the same medicine: the only medicine that leads to life. Hearts that, in the midst of darkness and sorrow, find repentance and enter into the fullness of divine communion—these are hearts that heal the world. The life of prayer, which leads to such repentant transfiguration into the life of God, is always the life that the world most needs; for it is the avenue that brings true Life to the very place where death seems to abound, and transforms it into something greater. Something that rises out of death. Something that gives up temporal sorrows for the eternal consolation of everlasting joy.

The life of prayer has always been, and will always be, the fundamental life of the Christian. Without prayer, we have no breath, no spiritual pulse. But when we learn to pray—even if we make only the most rudimentary beginning, fumbling over ourselves and struggling like children—revived breath comes into our lungs and our blood starts to flow anew. Our soul tastes of uncreated, holy things, the very things that have always been meant to be our "food and drink" as children of God our Creator; and from this first taste the soul longs ever after for more. It is prayer that lifts us up and calls us to higher things; and by the Lord's mysterious love, it is itself the means by which these things come to us.

As always, the means to this higher Life in Christ are eminently practical. Prayer is amongst the deepest theological mysteries of the heart, of the intercommunion of God and man; yet it is not the reserve of only the rightly educated, the sufficiently intellectual. It is the pathway into the Kingdom of God that is open to all, accessible to the old and the young, the wise and the simple. If we are to attain it, we must make a beginning: a good, solid beginning that starts with taking stock of our lives, recognizing our true spiritual condition, and then receiving the guidance from the Church for the steps we must take from there—the steps that will lead us from where we are, wherever we are, to the greater ascents of spiritual life. These steps are often eminently practical, seemingly "basic," but they lead us to great heights, if only we will follow them!

It is my renewed hope, as this book sees its second printing, that all who read it will be inspired by the timeless teaching of the Church, and not put off by my own shortcomings, truly to make a new beginning each day in the life of prayer. The Kingdom of God is close to hand. Christ stands at the door of our hearts and knocks.

It is time to answer!

Bishop Irenei
December 6/19, 2016
Feast of St. Nicholas the Wonderworker

PART I

Taking Stock of Our Struggle

Icon of Christ "Not Made by Hands."
Tikhvin, Russia, sixteenth century, now located in the St. Petersburg
Russian State Museum.

The Call of Christ toward Self-Examination

Be attentive to yourself.[1] That is, observe yourself carefully from every side. Let the eye of your soul be sleepless to guard you. You walk in the midst of snares.[2] Hidden traps have been set by the enemy in many places. Therefore observe everything, *that you may be saved like a gazelle from traps and like a bird from snares.*[3]

—St. Basil the Great[4]

C HRIST CALLS US to take stock of our condition daily. The examination of thoughts, the confession of sins: these are integral to the ascetical life, to growth into the Kingdom. To cease the continual self-examination of the heart is to fall prey to the suicidal lethargy of the human race in its sinful condition: content in its self-will, satisfied with its current state—whatever that may be—and uninterested in the hard work of transformation in Christ.

A truly Christian life, a life that seeks prayer and transfiguration in Christ, is one that continually examines itself, seeing its weakness and seeking a way out of its bondage to sin. Aware of the finitude of this earthly existence, of the inevitable parting of the soul from the body that is the cessation of the personal struggle of our created life, the Christian person must live day-to-day in the willful struggle of ascetical renewal. It is a struggle of hope, for the Lord promises the Kingdom to those who would *take it*

---

[1] Deuteronomy 15:9.

[2] Cf. Sirach 9:13.

[3] Proverbs 6:5.

[4] St. Basil the Great, *Homily on the Words "Be Attentive to Yourself,"* 2; in *St. Basil the Great: On the Human Condition,* trans. Nonna Verna Harrison (Crestwood, N.Y.: St. Vladimir's Seminary Press, 2005), p. 95.

by force[5] and assures each person of His continuous presence in that struggle: *I am with you always, even until the end of the age.*[6] And as He further assures, success in the struggle against sin and corruption, which is an impossibility to our frail and weakened nature, is nonetheless a real possibility through the grace of the Lord: for *those things which are impossible with men are possible with God,*[7] to which the Apostle adds, *I can do all things through Him Who gives me strength.*[8]

The impossible which is made possible in Christ is the confrontation with the passions: the head-on meeting with sin in the human heart, in all its members, by the frail person weakened in the spiritual contest. Apart from the power of Him Who makes weakness into strength, this is a senseless battle. The weakened man stands before what the Scriptures call "the strong man,"[9] and sees the mighty power of a tireless foe. Made frail by his infirmity, weakened to his bones by his long bondage to sin and complete submission to the passions, this man has no power before his enemy. As in the words of humbled Manasseh, he cries only *I am weighed down by many an iron fetter, I am rejected because of my sins, and I have no relief.*[10] He is made a slave to his enemy and cries out, *The troubles of my heart have enlarged.... See my distress!*[11]

Or so he ought. The depth of man's captivity to sin is so great, his tragedy so profound, that if he were to be aware of even a portion of its reality, such cries would consume his heart. And while such an awareness might be, for its time, the

---

[5] Matthew 11:12.

[6] Matthew 28:20.

[7] Luke 18:27.

[8] Philippians 4:13.

[9] Cf. Mark 3:22–29.

[10] Prayer of Manasseh, v. 10; see below, *A Century on Prayer and Watchfulness* §37, p. 82.

[11] Psalm 24:17–18.

source of great pain, this pain would at least bind him more fully to the work of Christ, for the Lord takes such tribulation and makes it into a strengthening ordeal, as iron is tested by fire and made stronger by it.[12]

Yet man is not bound to Christ in this way, because he little admits, little recognizes, the true condition of his heart. The chains of his bondage and the shackles of his slavery have become so commonplace, so "normal," that they are no longer seen. The passions have become such familiar and commonplace enemies that man loses sight of their true character, their oppressive nature, and even starts to consider them friends. The enemy which ceaselessly wages war against him is so much a "part of the fabric" that he ceases to be seen at all; his existence begins even to be denied, to be "rationalized" into a psychological context that makes him a thing unreal, unimposing, remote. So the spiritual struggle becomes a non-struggle, which makes it a defeat; for if we do not recognize our state, we cease to rise to the contest in full seriousness and vigor—and then our passions reign, sin triumphs, and the devil stakes a firmer claim. We then become like the spiritually idle brother who approached St. Anthony the Great of Egypt in the desert:

> A brother came to Abba Anthony and said, "Pray for me." The old man replied to him, "I will have no mercy upon you, nor will God have any, if you yourself do not make an effort and do not pray to God."[13]

This is the hopeless state to which spiritual lethargy leads: one in which man does not struggle, does not act. So he fails to attain even the fundamentals of the true Life in Christ. While modern man in some ways feels himself "enlightened" by no

(margin note: rationalized into oblivion)

---

[12] Cf. Psalm 65:10; Isaiah 48:10; Malachi 3:2.

[13] St. Anthony the Great, Saying 16; in *The Sayings of the Desert Fathers: The Alphabetical Collection,* ed. Benedicta Ward (Kalamazoo, Mich.: Cistercian Publications, 1975; revised edition, 1984), p. 4.

longer subscribing to the old-fashioned legends and myths of the devil, demons, spiritual contest or, at times, even sin itself, the Christian knows this enlightenment to be pure delusion. It is the hiding of reality beneath the thin veil of "knowing better"—a veil that is transparent when one looks at it objectively from the Church's perspective of true knowledge in the Lord; yet which, without that knowledge, seems to many to be the very fabric of reality itself.

How hopeless this all would seem, were it not for the reality of the resurrected Christ! Without this, man's very existence would be defined by but one word: death. All his sin, all his willing submission to the passions, leads only there. The work of his enemy strives to bring about this one fruit. Man's inability to recognize his weakness and the strength of his foes would assure their success. This would be truly a cause for despair—for true sorrow and lamentation.

But the Christian person, even the whole created race of man, has been offered the one thing needful: the defeat of death itself. By this defeat, wrought by Christ at the Cross, in the tomb, and in hades in His self-sacrificing glory, the contest in which man is engaged is one preceded by the emblems of victory. The Cross is made the ensign of life, and the battleground of the heart is reclaimed for glory in the risen Lord.

This does not mean that the contest ceases. The devil may be defeated, but he still wields a powerful sword. We still bow down before the passions; but redemption has come to the race of man. The contest is renewed and given strength in Christ. The Spirit has come to provide the armor of the battle. Weakness is made powerful and the impossible is made possible for the human race in its Lord.

So our daily task is great: to look inward, to the depth of the heart, to discover there the chains that bind us deep to the bottommost parts of the sea, and by the grace of Christ to struggle against them. We are called to work, through the redemptive power of the incarnate Lord, to defeat that which seeks our destruction. We are to take stock of our condition daily, to see it in its true weakness, and to call upon the solace and support of the charitable Lord to overcome it.

We are called to change, to be transformed: to see and know ourselves, so that we can offer ourselves to Christ for transfiguration.

THE CALL OF THE WORLD

The world, however, often calls us to a different task, for the mantra of society is largely one of self-satisfaction. It is true that by this world we are called, at times, to examine ourselves; but we are usually charged to do so in order to discover how to be happy and content with ourselves, either as we are or with the "true self" that is an expansion and clarification of this present existence. This worldly self-examination is of a predictably humanist, fatalist sort: humanity is at its best when it comes to be "content with itself" as it is, deep within. We are to look inwards, to discover and define the "self" with whom we must learn to be comfortable and content.

This call takes different forms in the modern world, but it can be reduced to essentially two. Firstly, there is the simplistic belief that one can and should be whatever one wishes to be, however one wishes to be it, so long as one does not harm others. Here one is called to change little, if at all; the goal of any self-examination is the discovery of the "me" with whom to be happy and satisfied. Such a basic worldview has been at the heart of various social trends, from the counter-cultural movements of the 1960s through to the universal acceptance mindsets of the current generation. It is, as it were, the most basic and extreme form of a "satisfaction now" belief system. Because it is fundamentally simple, it is rarely expanded upon in any detail: the very core of such a mindset is that any attempt to particularize belief and action imposes upon the freedom of the will in a negative way.

A more nuanced, refined form exists, however, in the various contours of the "new age" and "self-help" movements, which are as popular in the first decades of the twenty-first century as they were in the twentieth. Here one encounters a wide variety of views, many of which are rather ornate but which still orbit around the central point of self-satisfaction and self-contentment. The difference between these philosophies and that of the simplistic "be-what-you-want-to-be" mindset is that they oftentimes do involve calls to change and transformation—even a transformation of the self. Such views espouse a degree of nuance: that between *false* self-love and *true* self-love, with the one being bound by flaws and problems, and the other being authentic and exalted. In this, there is some glimmer of the authentic nature of self-examination that undergirds Orthodox ascesis: an examination revealing a disfigured vision of the human person. Talk of natural emotive states (such as shame) misused and abused also reflects, in some ways, a view of the perversion of nature that Orthodoxy identifies as the passions. There is a direct call for self-assessment and change, so that the false self, being lived at present and trapped in the shackles of various problems, can be shed in favor of the true self, which is the ready object of love.

Beneath this outwardly ascetical form, however (for this is indeed a kind of secular ascesis), there remains a solid foundation in self-definition. The "true self" one aims to discover and love is still a self defined by one's will and desires. So while this is more nuanced and complex than the simple "be-what-you-want-to-be, as-you-are-now, so-long-as-you-do-not-harm-others" mindset, the root of both is the same: satisfaction gained through contentment in the self, as defined by the self.

How great is this temptation, and how pervasive is this worldview! Yet this all-encompassing system of self-idolization can be readily identified as the fruit reared by the tree of a purely secular worldview. Let us remember that the root of this term,

↦ contempory

"secular," is the Latin *saeculum*: "generation" or "age," used in Christian vocabulary to mean "worldly," or bound up in the circumstances of the world in any given age. A secular worldview is one that sees the world, and human life within it, primarily or wholly in terms of "the things of this age"—of worldly viewpoints separated from the theological vision of the Church. This is the mindset that sees sin more and more as an outdated conviction of moral behavior; demons as old-fashioned, superstitious jargon used to describe what the world now "knows" to be simply psychological factors; heaven and hell as outmoded myths aimed at enforcing moral codes; and the thoughts currently in favor amongst a lost generation as the ultimate truths that must drive and define human existence.

It is little wonder, then, that such a worldview would call the person toward a different kind of self-examination than that demanded by Christ. Without an acknowledgment that this world is the work of a Creator, that it is the venue of growth for a creature who has an opponent in that growth, that it is moving toward judgment, redemption, and renewal—without these things, the impetus for a call to *genuine change into the sanctifying life of the Creator* is easily lost. Rather, when the world and this life are seen as ends in themselves, when this life and this "self" are understood to be the sole, defining contours of existence (and even of "god"), the impetus is toward *acceptance*. One must accept things as they are, and so find contentment. This is true even in the systems which advocate change in one's self-perception and definition; for a change from one mode of self-definition to another (even if the latter may in some ways be less problematic than the former) is but a movement within a common context. One is still finding contentment through accepting the idol of the self, even if one is being told to reshape that picture of the self before accepting it.

This mentality is a deception and a trap to the Christian, and it behooves us to be aware of just how insidious it is in society

self-help books

names are given to us, not self-defined

not to say that one should't better themselve but rather that they should't be content w/ themselves today. We live in the "self-help generation," where the do-it-yourself mentality is applied to the inner life as much as the outer; and the divorce of struggles relating to the inner life from the counsel of the Church means that the goals set for such "help" are often simply the fruits and desires of whoever happens to be writing the latest book, offering the latest wisdom. But the overarching principle remains one of satisfaction. The human person is charged not to become something else (except inasmuch as he may be prompted to shed certain attributes which keep him from being who he really is at his core), but to become happy with the self that currently lies hidden. What are to be shed are those things others seek to "impose" on us; for these are things which "deny the true self," which "seek conformity" to "someone else's morality," and thus prevent a true contentment with one's own being. And so the popular social program, which also influences domineering political movements, is one of renewed self-contentment: of claiming as right that which conforms to my view of "self," whatever this may happen to be and however I may come to arrive at it.

How far this is from the Christian calling! It is, at its best, deeply discordant. At its worst (and we often see it at its worst), it is utterly antithetical. Christianity is a life rooted in Christ's own. Its charge is not to live for self but to live for Christ; and its goal is not satisfaction but transformation. The Christian is called to *become,* to enter into a *newness* of life *that is another's— that is Christ's.* He is to discover the "self" of his current existence, *precisely so that he can work to change it* into a life not defined by his will, but defined and made real by another—by God Himself. The Life in Christ is a life of transformation into a New Man. It is a life that works toward resurrection, when *the body of this death*[14] shall pass away and the glorified man will know the Lord of Glory.

---

[14] Romans 7:24.

The Christian today hears two calls: that of God, and that of the world. And truly, this is as it has always been, since Christ first spoke into the world the Gospel that sets *father ... against son,... mother against daughter,*[15] and the Kingdom against the *saeculum.* The constant temptation is to answer both, as if both were of equal value, or of a value that could be held hand-in-hand with the other; but this is to ignore the word of the Lord. *Let the dead bury their own dead*[16] was a statement uttered by Christ not as a cold, uncaring dismissal of the world, but in order to teach His disciples that the call of a world that leads to death must be left to respond to itself. The call to the Kingdom must be the sole focus of the Christian heart. Only by responding to this call, and this call alone, can a man truly be merciful to "the dead"—to those who are lost in sin, who succumb to the call of the world—for the only antidote to death is resurrection, and resurrection comes only through the power of the risen Lord.

---

[15] Luke 12:53.
[16] Matthew 8:22; Luke 9:60.

Attending to Our Struggles

CONFORMING OUR VISION TO THE WELLSPRING OF LIFE

H OW, THEN, are we to respond authentically to the heavenly call of the Holy Trinity? How are we to take up the Apostolic life of true and complete adherence to the Gospel of Christ, which may save us from death and unite us to the joy that knows no end?

The task of the Christian today is not simply to engage in the necessary self-examination that enables authentic, beneficial spiritual struggle; it is, beyond this, to reclaim the very realities that define that struggle from the reductionist mindset of the world around him. The Christian today—not unlike Christians of other eras, but in ways that are continually "updated" as society carries on—is not told simply that he mustn't fight the passions, that he mustn't battle the devil: he is told that the passions are unreal, that the devil does not exist. He is told that ascesis is unnatural, that spiritual warfare is delusional. He is told that judgment is oppressive and the desire to become something defined by another (even God!) is psychologically unhealthy. He is told that to believe in the Church's tradition is a simplistic, pietistic adherence to the past; that he had better "think for himself."

He is told, in other words, that the very arena of the spiritual contest is unreal, and that his work is foolishness. He is made to believe that the only way it can be defended at all in modern society is for it to be conformed to society's views.

He is told, we might say, precisely what the devil would want him to be told.

The Christian today, then, is charged with a mission: to reclaim from this disastrous situation the right contours of truth and reality, and to live them fully despite the world's constant insistence to do otherwise. The Christian must reclaim, firstly in himself (this, the ascetical struggle), and then with an eye to and for those around him, the right vision of our condition in this life and our approach to it.

look out!

How are we to do this? The only way is by renewing in ourselves the ascetical vision handed on to us in the Church, and by conforming ourselves to the life that binds us to the wellspring of life, Christ Himself. Given the degree to which the world etches itself into our minds and hearts, this means at a basic and practical level that we must struggle inwardly to reclaim that which the Church unfailingly provides, so that our own struggle is built up by the true bulwark of the Faith.

In practical terms, this may be accomplished through a renewed attentiveness to the true contours of our ascetical struggle: firstly, we must refocus our vision on the Kingdom. Secondly, we must redevelop in ourselves an awareness of our enemies: the devil and the demons. Thirdly, we must come to understand more directly the nature of the passions. Fourthly, we must continually relearn the nature and practice of obedience. And fifthly, we must work to bear a better, stronger witness in the world.

REFOCUSING OUR VISION ON THE KINGDOM OF GOD

Seek first the Kingdom of God and His righteousness, and all these things will be added unto you.[1]

If there is one overarching debasement of the Christian vision in our days, it is in the loss of a constant gaze upon the future life of man in the Kingdom. The focus of the *saeculum,* of the secular world, is upon the now. *This* moment, *this* world, *this* life:

---

[1] Matthew 6:33.

these are the contexts of meaning. While the Christian may often acknowledge the Kingdom, may even speak of its attainment and its nature, how rarely today does an orientation of all life and living around and toward this Kingdom actually manifest itself, even among the baptized. Rather, the Kingdom of God is often taken as a kind of "backdrop" by which one can give a Christian flavor to the present. "I shall do such-and-such now, because such an act is loving, and the Kingdom of God is a kingdom of love." Or, "I shall seek this good now, rather than that, because God's Kingdom focuses on such aims." It is not that there is no nobility in such reflections (certainly, they are better than a view which takes no account at all of the Kingdom); but the Christian life demands more than this. Christ does not say, "When you consider this life, remember the Kingdom and so let it inform what you seek"; rather, He commands: *Seek first the Kingdom of God and His righteousness.* Only after He has given this sole and primary focus to Christian endeavor, does He add: *and all these things will be added unto you.*

The Kingdom of God is, in the words of St. Maximus the Confessor, "the consummation of created things" and the full and complete "imparting through grace of those blessings which pertain naturally to God."[2] In the words of St. Theodoros the Great Ascetic, it is the human beholding of the Holy Trinity, by which "what is lacking and imperfect in us is supplied and perfected."[3] This Kingdom is the full communion of the creature in its Creator—the life of ultimate blessedness toward which all redeemed creation is moving, toward which God calls the penitent. Christ's call is not for man occasionally to remember the Kingdom toward which he strives, and to have

---

[2] St. Maximus the Confessor, *Second Century on Theology,* 90; in the *Philokalia,* vol. 2, ed. Kallistos Ware et al. (London: Faber and Faber, 1981), p. 161.

[3] St. Theodoros the Great Ascetic, *Theoretikon;* in the *Philokalia,* vol. 2, p. 43.

that remembrance give some shape to his day-to-day life in this world. His call is for man to be *wholly shaped and formed by the seeking of the Kingdom.* The object of the Christian's vision is at every moment to be the Kingdom of God. The focus of every deliberation, of every act, of every thought and movement of the heart is to be God's righteousness, which shows forth and makes accessible this Kingdom. Any aspect of life which is focused otherwise, which takes as its compass and measure something other than this struggle toward the Kingdom, is to be regarded as part of the "old life" of the "old man."[4] Such things bind us to what is fleeting, while Christ has come to call us to what is eternal.

In commenting upon the Lord's words in St. Matthew's account of the Gospel, the great orator and pastor St. John of Constantinople, the "Golden-mouthed," offered the following counsel:

> [The Lord] came to do away with the old things, and to call us to a greater country. Therefore He does all, to deliver us from things unnecessary and from our affection for the earth. For this cause He mentioned the heathens also, saying that *the Gentiles seek after these things*[5]—they whose whole labor is for the present life, who have no regard for the things to come, nor any thought of heaven. But to you the chief things are not these which are present, but other than these. For we were not born for this end, that we should eat and drink and be clothed, but that we might please God, and attain unto the good things to come. Therefore as things here are secondary in our labor, so also in our prayers let them be secondary. Therefore He also said, *Seek the Kingdom of Heaven, and all these things shall be added unto you.*[6]

---

4 Cf. Romans 6:6; Ephesians 4:22; Colossians 3:9.

5 Matthew 6:32.

6 St. John Chrysostom, *Homilies on St. Matthew's Gospel*, 22.4. Cf. Nicene and Post-Nicene Fathers, 1st series, vol. 10, p. 153.

The Christian's orientation is toward "a greater country" than this present life. Our birth is not for the pleasures of this world and its fleeting comforts, but for the glory of God and the attainment of His Kingdom.

If we are to struggle authentically toward our sanctification and redemption, this orientation toward and into the Kingdom must become paramount in us. Every act must be considered from the perspective of that future life and its attainment. When we do not act in such a way, we reduce our choices and our behaviors to the limited perspective of this brief sojourn. Rather than see the context of our behaviors, actions, and decisions as the eternal life of God's abiding Kingdom, we see it as the short span of this life and adjust our whole vision and worldview accordingly.

If we assess our condition honestly, we see that this is precisely what is so often done. How many of our choices in life are made based on considerations of existence, defined solely as life between birth and the grave! When we plan for the future, we most often mean our later years—our adulthood, our old age. We struggle after benefits of health that will add a few days to this life, for we take death to be the end. Again, this is very often true even among those who are baptized *into the eternal life of Christ*, into the unending Kingdom of eternity. This limited vision, which traps the human person into the present life, separates us from the true calling of that eternal home. We come even to make moral determinations based on the short scope of this life and its comforts. And while we acknowledge—perhaps—the Kingdom, we do so in a manner that sets it as a "second thing," after the affairs of the present age. We seek an acknowledgment of the Kingdom that provides a way for God to give us, and for us to obtain, the things of this world. But on this approach, St. John Chrysostom also speaks:

> The Lord said not [that the things of this world] "shall be given," but *shall be added*, that you might learn that the things

present are no great part of His gifts, compared with the greatness of the things to come. Accordingly, He does not bid us so much as ask for them, but while we ask for other things, to have confidence, as though these also were added to those. Seek then the things to come, and you will receive the things present also; seek not the things that are seen, and you shall surely attain unto them. Yea, for it is unworthy of you to approach your Lord for such things. And you, who ought to spend all your zeal and your care for those unspeakable blessings, do greatly disgrace yourself by consuming it on the desire for transitory things.[7]

The *sole focus* of the Christian's attention, as St. John perceives the Lord's words, must be on Christ's Kingdom and His righteousness. Then may the Lord *add to this struggle for the Kingdom* certain blessings of this world; yet those blessings are but the flowering of His divine support for the eternal struggle. A life lived in the struggle toward the Kingdom is one in which God will add to the contest such things as are needful while we are in this world—yet to approach the Lord for such things, or to orient our own minds and hearts around them as even secondary or concordant aims, is to "greatly disgrace" ourselves, consuming our desire with the fleeting things of this life.

Such words reveal to us the disgrace of so much of our behavior today. Not only do we seek the things of this world: we also allow our theological vision to be shaped by our this-worldly focus. In this vein, such things as authentic renunciation, true asceticism, real self-abasement, and true self-sacrifice cease to "make sense," for they do not conform to a vision of life that is primarily oriented toward the present.

As such, the Christian must rise up and reclaim the right vision of the Kingdom and orient the whole of his life toward it. Our every thought, our every action, must be steeped in the

---

7 Ibid.

vision of this divine life, so that by this vision we can effect some change in this world; for to seek the Kingdom is not to dismiss the world: it is to reclaim the only orientation that can redeem it. But we must begin by acknowledging, at the very depth of our being, the true reality of this Kingdom; and we must start by calling it to mind frequently—at every moment—so that our lives are shaped by it, drawn toward it, and by God's grace gradually transfigured into it. We must seek to live our Christian lives after the manner of those Christians recounted by the anonymous first- or second-century writer of the Epistle to Diognetus:

> The Christians are distinguished from other men neither by country, nor language, nor the customs which they observe; for they neither inhabit cities of their own, nor employ a particular form of speech, nor lead a way of life marked out by any singular worldly attribute of life.... But, inhabiting Greek as well as barbarian cities, according as the lot of each of them has determined, and following the local customs with respect to clothing, food, and the rest of their ordinary conduct, they display to us their wonderful and confessedly striking manner of life. They dwell in their own countries, but simply as sojourners. As citizens, they share in all things with others, and yet endure all things as foreigners. Every foreign land is to them as their native country, and every land of their birth a land of strangers.... They are in the flesh, but they do not live after the flesh. They pass their days on earth, but they are citizens of heaven. They obey the prescribed laws, and at the same time surpass the laws by their lives. They love all men, though they are persecuted by all. They are unknown, yet condemned; they are put to death, yet they are restored to life. They are poor, yet they make many rich. They lack and are in want of all things, yet they abound in all; they are dishonored, and yet in their very dishonor they are glorified.[8]

"They dwell in their own countries, but simply as sojourn-

---

[8] *Epistle to Diognetus,* 5.

ers." This is the otherworldly life of the Kingdom that manifests itself in authentic Christian living. The only focus of such a one as could fit this exalted description is that eternal Kingdom—the very reality which makes it a trivial thing to be continually a foreigner, to be persecuted, to be unknown, condemned, to be ever in want in this earthly sojourn. These are but minor things for one who "passes his days on earth, but is a citizen of heaven." And, far from this orientation toward the Kingdom being a thing that abandons God's creation, it is something that has real power to transform it. It is such a one "who is poor, *yet makes many rich*."

Orthodox Christians today must reclaim this focus. It stands at the heart and center of the whole Life in Christ. As explained by St. Innocent of Alaska:

> Jesus Christ, the Son of God, came to this world in order to return to us our lost immortal life and true happiness. He revealed to people that all their evil lies in sin and that no one through their own efforts can overcome the evil within themselves and attain communion with God. Sin, ingrained in our nature since the fall, stands between us and God like a high wall. If the Son of God had not descended to us through His mercy for us, had not taken on our human nature, and had not by His death conquered sin, all mankind would have perished for ever! Now, thanks to Him, those who wish to cleanse themselves from evil can do so and return to God and obtain eternal bliss in the Kingdom of Heaven.[9]

REDEVELOPING IN OURSELVES AN AWARENESS OF OUR ENEMIES

He that committeth sin is of the devil; for the devil sinneth from the beginning.[10]

---

[9] St. Innocent of Alaska, *The Indication of the Way into the Kingdom of Heaven*, 1.

[10] I John 3:8.

He was a murderer from the beginning, and abode not in the truth, because there is no truth in him. When he speaketh a lie, he speaketh of his own: for he is a liar and the father of it.[11]

Satan stood up against Israel, and provoked David to number Israel.[12]

When the unclean spirit is gone out of a man, he walketh through dry places seeking rest, and he findeth none. Then he saith, I will return into my house from whence I came out; and when he is come, he findeth it empty, swept, and garnished. Then goeth he, and taketh with himself seven other spirits more wicked than himself, and they enter in and dwell there: and the last state of that man is worse than the first.[13]

It is sometimes said that the devil's greatest ruse is to convince man that he does not exist. Yet this is more than an axiom or witty saying: it is one of the most telling truths of our day and one of the most critical dimensions of our captivity, which must be overcome if we are to live the Christian life authentically and fully.

That there is a devil, that there are demons, and that these beings wage an active war against mankind and its salvation is so foundational a testimony of the Church that it is shocking it needs clarifying among Christians; yet too often it does. The Holy Scriptures, of both covenants, are filled with testimony to demonic powers, to the demons and their activities, and to the chief among them: the devil, given the name Satan ("the Apostate"). They are known to be fallen spirits: ranks of the angelic orders in rebellion and apostasy—those who, following their instigator, *fell as lightning from heaven.*[14] They are known to be

---

[11] John 8:44.
[12] I Paraleipomenon (I Chronicles) 21:1.
[13] Matthew 12:43–45.
[14] Cf. Luke 10:18.

the chief sources of sin and death (*through the devil's envy, death entered the world*),[15] and the rulers over debased evil in the world they have so captivated (*the rulers of the darkness of this world*).[16]

This knowledge of a cosmos inhabited not only by our material ranks but also by the immaterial—both Godly and rebellious—is the same knowledge confirmed and conferred by the incarnate Lord. It is Christ Who assures His disciples that suffering comes from the demons; healing involves the overcoming of demonic power and the casting out of demonic presence. Much of the Lord's earthly ministry was consumed with the casting out of demons; and often Christ's instruction on prayer and Christian living was framed precisely in the context of overcoming Satan and his ranks. When the apostles are unable to heal a suffering epileptic, Jesus' instruction is to orient prayer and ascesis, and indeed the very power of faith, around true demonic exorcism: *This kind does not come out but by prayer and fasting.*[17]

Christ's work in this world, during the period of His first earthly sojourn as man (for He shall come again as man to judge both the living and the dead), was centered on combatting Satan and his demonic forces. Subsequent to His Baptism in the Jordan, the first we see of Christ's ministerial life is His temptation in the desert by this devil.[18] Throughout His earthly life, He was continually active in identifying demonic presence, casting out demons, and providing His disciples with the means to do the same.

If this is Christ's work in His human life, can the Christian's possibly be anything else? Yet how often does an active awareness of the devil and the demons infuse Christian life and behavior in our day? So out of fashion is any belief in the demonic side of the

---

[15] Wisdom 2:24.
[16] Ephesians 6:12.
[17] Matthew 17:21.
[18] Cf. Matthew 4:1–11; Mark 1:12–13; Luke 4:1–13.

spiritual realm, that many Christians are content to admit that the demons are simply old-fashioned myths used to explain suffering, illness, evil, and the like; it is not even considered that they might be real beings, with wills and intentions bent on the upset of man's life. Should the existence of the devil be admitted at all, he is construed as a kind of generic personification of evil and all that is against God: but again, this is oftentimes articulated in a manner that aims simply to identify that the force of good has a counterpart, but not as a genuine confession of a being with an identity, a will, an intention, and an active engagement in our lives as human beings.

In the understanding of the Orthodox Church, this is quite simply the deceptive work of the devil himself. As St. Irenaeus of Lyons wrote in the mid-second century, the devil "is long accustomed to lie against God, for the purpose of leading men astray."[19] This deception, this "leading astray," is nowhere more prominent in our day than in the widespread conviction that there are no such things as demons and that Satan is but a legendary metaphor for psychological trauma and weakness.

In Christ's own words, however, *he was a murderer from the beginning, and abode not in the truth, because there is no truth in him.*[20] Not only do the devil and the demons exist, the Lord confirms, but they are the active opponents of humankind. The devil is the "murderer" of souls, leading them into apostasy from God—but ultimately not only of souls, but bodies as well; for when we rebel against the Creator, our whole created nature moves toward corruption and death.

The Church teaches, clearly and soberly, that the demonic realm is a reality and that it is not wholly a mystery to man (though it is not wholly known either; it remains a mystery

---

[19] St. Irenaeus of Lyons, *On the Refutation and Overthrow of Knowledge Falsely So-Called* (commonly known as *Against Heresies*), 5.23.1.

[20] John 8:44.

into which man has gazed). The devil himself is known by name; rather, by several names—"Lucifer," "Satan," "the Tempter," "Beelzebub," etc. The ranks of the angels who followed him in his apostasy are known to have been cast out of the Kingdom, and to exist now in the ethereal or aerial realms, as well as in hades itself. The Fathers consistently proclaim their "territory" as chiefly that of the air: so the devil is known as "the prince of the power of the air";[21] the demons are "the spirits of wickedness under the heavens."[22] They are active in the spiritual struggle, waging ever-fiercer battle against those who take up the Christian life with seriousness.[23] As was written in the middle of the nineteenth century by a great ascetical bishop, St. Ignatius(Brianchaninov):

> Although the demons, in appearing to men, usually assume the appearance of bright angels in order to deceive the more easily; although they strive sometimes to convince men that they are human souls and not demons (this manner of deception at the present time is in special fashion among demons, due to the particular disposition of contemporary men to believe it); even though they sometimes foretell the future;[24]

---

[21] Ephesians 2:2.

[22] Ephesians 6:12.

[23] In the words of St. John of Kronstadt, "The devil is in the habit of attacking us when we are in straitened circumstances" (from *My Life in Christ,* in *The Spiritual Counsels of Father John of Kronstadt,* ed. W. Jardine Grisbrooke [Crestwood, N.Y.: St. Vladimir's Seminary Press, 1967/1981], p. 109). So too, St. John Climacus: "An active soul is a provocation to the demons; yet the greater the conflicts, the greater our rewards" (*The Ladder of Divine Ascent,* Step 26: "On Discernment," in *John Climacus: The Ladder of Divine Ascent,* ed. and trans. Colin Luibheid and Norman Russell [New York: Paulist Press, 1982], p. 251).

[24] Here St. Ignatius speaks somewhat in shorthand, dealing in the practical matters of apparent realities rather than attempting a definition of the powers of the demons. The Fathers are, as a whole, quite clear that the demons do not in fact have an authentic awareness of future events, lacking as they do

even though they reveal mysteries—still one must not trust them in any way whatsoever. With them the truth is mixed with falsehood; truth is used at times only for a more convenient deception.[25]

In this counsel, which is all but of our modern day, St. Ignatius reflects the vision of the Fathers from the first days of the Church of Christ. St. Irenaeus had identified, as we have already seen, the devil's main tool in leading men astray as that of deception; and later he added that "as therefore the devil lied at the beginning, so did he also in the end"—lying to Eve in Eden, and to Christ in the desert.[26] In St. Ignatius' counsel, he carries on the tone of his own forebear in Christ, St. Ignatius of Antioch, who in the first or earliest second century had written: "I put you on your guard, inasmuch as I love you greatly, and foresee the snares of the devil."[27]

If we are to take stock of our lives and our genuine condition, and if we are to engage more wholly in the transfiguring ascetical life that leads into the Kingdom, we must redevelop in ourselves an awareness of our adversary—to come ourselves to "foresee the snares of the devil." To follow Christ is to know the power of this enemy, of the demons, and to work actively against them even as

---

the omniscience and foreknowledge proper to God. Their seeming foreknowledge is a show, intended to deceive man. In the words of St. John Climacus on the apparent foreknowledge of the devil, "Because he is a spiritual being, he knows what is happening in the lower regions, that someone is dying, for instance; so by way of dreams he passes on the information to the more gullible. However, demons lack actual foreknowledge. If they did not, these tricksters would be able to foretell our deaths" (St. John Climacus, *Ladder*, Step 3: On Exile, "Concerning the dreams of novices," p. 89).

[25] St. Ignatius (Brianchaninov), Bishop of the Black Sea and the Caucasus, *Collected Works* [in Russian], vol. 3 (Jordanville, N.Y.: Holy Trinity Monastery, 1985), pp. 7–9.

[26] St. Irenaeus, *Refutation* 5.24.1. Cf. Genesis 3:1–4; Matthew 4:9; Luke 4:6.

[27] St. Ignatius of Antioch, *Epistle to the Trallians*, 8.

they work actively against us. The world constantly tries to pull this perspective from the Christian's view, to "de-demonize" the spiritual life and struggle; but this is always to bleed the very life from that contest. One cannot wage a battle if one does not acknowledge the existence of an enemy; and the Church's testimony is clear, that whether or not one acknowledges that foe, whether or not one elects to fight in the battle, the foe remains real and never ceases in his attacks against us. So our choice is not "to fight or not to fight," to acknowledge the demons or not to admit of their reality; our choice is to fight or to be overcome.

In this, we find the contours of authentic Christian struggle as it has been defined and articulated in the Church from the very beginning. We see this clearly in a text from the fifth century by St. Diadochus of Photiki: *won't be held captive*

> Captivity is one thing; battle is another. Captivity signifies a violent abduction, while battle indicates a contest between equally matched adversaries. For precisely this reason the Apostle says that the devil attacks with fiery arrows those who carry Christ in their souls. For someone who is not at close grips with his enemy uses arrows against him, attacking from a distance. In the same way, when, because of the presence of grace, Satan can lurk no longer in the *nous*[28] of those pursuing a spiritual way, he lurks instead in the body and exploits its members, so that through its proclivities he may seduce the soul. We should therefore weaken the body to some extent, so

---

[28] *Nous* is a technical term of the Christian ascetical vocabulary and is notoriously difficult to translate. While it is sometimes rendered "intellect" in English, this leaves open the door for viewing it as meaning simply man's rational faculty or intellectual knowledge. There is more to the term than this. It might also be translated "heart," when this is taken in the ascetical sense of the seat of man's life and knowing; but here, too, there are problems, since the nous and heart are distinct terms in Orthodox ascetical vocabulary. I have elected to keep the term untranslated, admittedly not an ideal solution, but one which might perhaps aid in drawing us into a contemplation of the deeper meaning and, ultimately, the mystery of man's interior dimension.

that the *nous* does not slide down the smooth path of sensual pleasure because of the body's humors.... Thus it is clear that the *nous* cannot be the common dwelling-place of both God and the devil.[29]

The modern man must open his eyes to the clear context of this early writing, which is so much in harmony with the whole testimony of Christ and the Fathers. The context of Christian struggle is the struggle against a foe—against the demons. This was a reality that caused an early desert-dweller to weep, shocked at the demons' fortitude. Struck by the devil's power even to provoke his body and physical environment—just as St. Diadochus, above, notes—Abba Elias of Scetis turned to Christ and explained his tears: "I weep, because the demons have dared to seize a man and treat him like this." Christ replied to the monk, "You had been careless. As soon as you turned to Me again, you see I was beside you." The lesson drawn in the account is clear: "I say this, because it is necessary to take great pains, and anyone who does not do so cannot come to his God—for He Himself was crucified for our sake."[30]

This is a particular challenge for modern man. To admit of the demons as actual beings, to confess the Christian struggle as an actual contest against demonic forces, is to present oneself for the scoffing of the world. The man who admits of this truth, the world will call naïve, simplistic. It will claim that he does not see the demons from the intellectual perspective of psychological identity—that he is trapped in old-fashioned views and unenlightened as to the more robust vision of theology today. Much of the world will simply tease him, and pour a kind of patronizing scorn on "that poor soul" who cannot escape the legends of

---

[29] St. Diadochus of Photiki, *On Spiritual Knowledge,* 82; in the *Philokalia,* vol. 1, ed. Kallistos Ware et al. (London: Faber and Faber, 1979), p. 283.

[30] Abba Elias, Saying 7; in *The Sayings of the Desert Fathers: The Alphabetical Collection,* pp. 71–72.

the past. The Christian who boldly confesses these truths today sets himself at odds with a mindset that simply does not understand the truth of creation in all its dimensions. The confession of this truth sets him up for mocking and ridicule.

Yet it is the only confession that prepares the human person for true spiritual growth. Without it, we do not engage in the same struggle as that lived by Christ, and as such cannot conform our lives wholly to His—for His was a life opposed to the demons and their power. What, then, shall my life be?

UNDERSTANDING THE NATURE OF THE PASSIONS

A right orientation toward the Kingdom of God sets the heart in the only position whereby it may accurately struggle in a Christ-like way in this world. Not only does the heart come to see its foe more directly—that is, the external spiritual realm which wages battle against the righteous—but it also is given the perspective to understand its own internal warfare. That is, an orientation of life past the sinful confines of this world, toward the eternity of the Kingdom, allows man to see his fallen self more authentically, discovering in himself those things which prevent him from conformity to Christ and growth into this Kingdom. These are what the Fathers call "the passions," and a right perception of them is essential in the ascetical struggle of the Christian.

Literally, the passions are those impulses of the soul, of the heart (and thus, also of the body), which it suffers "passively" (hence the Greek *pathos* and Latin *passio*). The Fathers understand this passive suffering in a negative sense: the passions are bound up in the *domination* of the soul by something other than the heart borne up in the love of God. The soul comes to be dominated by experiences which might, in another form, have a positive character (such as love, which can be divine; or anger, which can be righteous),[31] but which in a particular manifestation become negative through their stripping the soul of its freedom—making it a slave to a stronger force. So the soul, rather than governing man, becomes a passive captive to those impulses which are the actual forces ruling his life; and the soul's movements and desires, rather than being directed toward God and the attainment of His Kingdom, are misdirected toward baser things.

There is a tendency, in our day, to confuse the passions with all expressive sentiment or emotion—reflective of the way "passion" is used in English to mean intense outpourings of oftentimes good emotions such as love, zeal, etc. Given such usage, the exceedingly negative view of the passions in the Fathers gives some cause for concern, and the patristic description of the highest spiritual state as that of "dispassion" is taken to imply a de-emotionalized rejection of all human feeling. This view makes it hard to receive the words of one of the great early writers on the spiritual life: "Dispassion and humility lead to spiritual knowledge. Without them, no one can see God."[32]

"Passion," however, refers particularly and specifically to *the passive domination of the person by the misdirected impulses of*

---

[31] Though on the exercise of "righteous anger" the Fathers and other patristic-era writers advise extreme caution. Evagrius of Pontus speaks of it as the tool by which the passions and demons are confronted, following the Psalmist's command: *Be angry, and do not sin* (Psalm 4:4). In such a case, this anger directed toward the passions and demons becomes "a useful medicine for the soul at times of temptation" (Evagrius of Pontus, *On Discrimination* 15; in the *Philokalia*, vol. 1, p. 47). Yet Evagrius immediately goes on to note that there is a "demon of anger" also, suggesting that the line between righteous and demonic anger is hard to negotiate. Most often the Fathers speak of anger as a passion, and thus a thing sinister, to be avoided; see the extended comments to this end in St. John Cassian, *On the Eight Vices:* "Anger," in the *Philokalia*, vol. 1, pp. 82–87.

[32] St. Hesychius the Priest, *On Watchfulness and Holiness*, 67, in the *Philokalia*, vol. 1, p. 174.

body and soul, and in this, the patristic testimony to the passions constitutes an important affirmation of the authentic relationship of creation and transgression. That which God creates, which includes the full feeling capabilities of man, such as his ability to love, feel joy and sorrow, is itself intrinsically good;[33] yet sin works its destruction precisely by *misusing* that which is good, to negative effect. Evil is not a substance or independent reality: it is the willful misuse and distortion of God's sacred creation. Identification of the passions does not denigrate the goodness of the human creature in all its emotive reality; rather, it affirms that goodness precisely by showing that it is the perversion of soul and body that makes man's feelings an oppressive force. It is our domination by our emotive capacities, along with their misuse, that is evil, that must be combatted.

Coming to understand the passions rightly is a critical need in the Christian life—and this is nowhere truer than in our present world, where the desires and impulses of the mind are often conceived of as good in themselves. "Love" is understood, too often today, as an impulse or compulsion, a longing for that which "feels good"; "joy" is equated with a frivolous happiness; "satisfaction" is paralleled to sensual and intellectual gratification. Such assertions are at times quite bold-faced in our world; at other times they are less obvious, buried within systems of self-awareness and self-help that give them a more scientific context and nuanced definition, but which fundamentally assert the same ideas, however refined. When this is the context

---

[33] It should be noted, however, that sorrow is a sacred reality in man as a condescension of God to human sin: Godly sorrow is that repentant spirit of contrition and compunction in the face of sin that mirrors God's own sorrow over man's transgression (cf. II Corinthians 7:10). Sorrow cannot be seen to be the intended experience of man in his first-created condition, before his sin, in the same manner as, for example, love; yet it remains true that the creature bearing God's image has in its capabilities the potential to sorrow over sin as did the Lord Himself.

of man's understanding of his inner life, and the way its goods and negatives are determined, it becomes ever more difficult to make any real progress in the ascetical contest—for, in the Christian vision of man, those things that the world often calls "good" in his emotional state are in fact known to be deceptions, traps, and pitfalls in the spiritual struggle.

The Church's view of the passions begins with the affirmation that the sinful condition of man makes them a real presence deep in the inner life of each person. As St. Hesychius writes:

> Many passions are hidden in the soul; they can be checked only when their causes are revealed.[34]

This is to say, the condition of this world in sin (the heritage of man's transgression) is one in which the natural impulses of the human soul, united to its body, are not ordered as they ought to be. Rather, they are ordered toward the gratification of desires—intellectual as well as physical, overwhelmed by self-love and the longing for satisfaction—which is the source of their dominating power.

This is made apparent from the account of man's first transgression in Eden, where the right ordering of creation was upset through sin and rebellion. In Adam and Eve are exemplified the nature of the passions as disfigurations of natural impulses:

> Eve is the first to teach us that sight, taste, and the other senses, when used without moderation, distract the heart from its remembrance of God. So long as she did not look with longing at the forbidden tree, she was able to keep God's commandment carefully in mind; she was still covered by the wings of divine love and thus was ignorant of her own nakedness. But after she had looked at the tree with longing,

---

[34] St. Hesychius, *On Watchfulness and Holiness,* 72, in the *Philokalia,* vol. I, p. 175.

touched it with ardent desire, and then tasted its fruit with active sensuality, she at once felt drawn to physical intercourse and, being naked, she concurred with her passion. All her desire was now to enjoy what was immediately present to her senses, and through the pleasant appearance of the fruit she involved Adam in her fall.[35]

By succumbing to sensory desire, rather than reigning over it by God's dominion, the heart of man is "distracted" from its true orientation in God and His Kingdom. St. Diadochus' text gives blatant testimony to the power of this impulse and this distraction to take control over the human heart: Eve quickly falls prey to it, and her desires become passionate—that is, they are made actors and leaders, and she herself is made passive. She is dominated. She no longer has full reign over her mind and her life; her desire changes, her impulses are oriented anew. This is the nature of man's passionate state, and of the passions themselves. And this makes the inner condition of man one in which the apparently "natural" desires of the soul are in fact passionate desires—that is, they are distortions that dominate, rather than pure realities that can be used to bear good fruit. So what appears as man's natural condition in this life is in fact his passionate state: the "norm" is domination, enslavement, debasement. *What are the things w/n me I must war against?*

The Church understands this "normal" condition of passionate existence to be one which pervades precisely through its apparent normality. Day to day, man barely notices his passions, for he is so accustomed to them. This begins to change, however, when he starts to take his spiritual life seriously. Certain passions are stirred up as specific, discrete things against which battle must be waged—rather than an overarching context of man's whole existence—when the spiritual life is genu-

---

[35] St. Diadochus, *On Spiritual Knowledge*, 56. Cf. the *Philokalia*, vol. 1, p. 269.

inely embraced and the Christian attempts to live a life ordered toward God's Kingdom.

There is, then, a direct connection between the activity of the passions and the ascetical, spiritual life. The more seriously one takes that life, that struggle, the more the passions are aroused out of a general context of man's existence, to specific impulses of rebellion that attack him. This is emphasized in another important text by St. Diadochus:

> Spiritual knowledge teaches us that, at the outset, the soul in pursuit of theology is troubled by many passions, above all by anger and hatred. This happens to it not so much because the demons are arousing these passions, as because it is making progress. So long as the soul is worldly minded, it remains unmoved and untroubled—however much it sees people trampling justice underfoot. Preoccupied with its own desires, it pays no attention to the justice of God. When, however, because of its disdain for this world and its love for God, it begins to rise above its passions, it cannot bear, even in its dreams, to see justice set at naught.[36]

St. Diadochus draws attention to the fact that the usual condition of the human person is one that is "worldly minded," making little or no progress in the spiritual life because it is preoccupied with the things of the world and with its own desires.[37] This is the condition of one's whole life being passionate, enslaved to the overarching domination of the soul and body by worldly bound deception. The person whose whole life is thus bound up and defined by passionate enslavement loses his perspective on himself, on his neighbor, and above all on God.

Serious attentiveness to the ascetical struggle, however,

---

[36] Ibid., 71, p. 277.

[37] As is noted often in the patristic heritage, this is evidence of man's "appetitive power"—the power of his desiring, longing, seeking—being disfigured. The powers of his soul are oriented awry.

draws one out of this worldly minded focus toward a vision of the Kingdom; it draws the person into the love of God and out of this condition of complete domination by the passions. In this ascent and struggle, the passions move from being the utterly familiar and hence almost unnoticed context of man's complete domination, to specific manifestations of the rebellion of soul and body. His focus on the Kingdom causes a focusing of the passions, their concentration. Since they are no longer given free reign over his whole person, to be the basic context of his whole existence, they become concentrated in focused impulses. St. Diadochus emphasizes that chief among these, particularly in the early stages of ascetical struggle, are anger and hatred—the very impulses that rebel against the love of God being engendered in the heart.

This is, as it were, the "natural" reaction of the human creature to ascetical growth. But it is also conditioned by the enemy of man, who uses the concentration of the passions that come about through serious spiritual struggle as a foundation on which to build additional hindrances to authentic growth.[38] This the demons accomplish, in the teaching of the Church, through the drawing of the heart toward the passions; the "sowing" in the heart of passions by which it can again be captivated; and the encouragement and strengthening of those passions to which the person proves particularly vulnerable.

This engagement of Satan and the demons with the focusing of the passions in a person who seriously engages in the ascetical life, is drawn out in numerous writings among the Fathers. Perhaps most clearly and simply, it is seen in a saying of Abba Matoes in the Egyptian desert:

> Abba Matoes said, "Satan does not know by what passion the soul can be overcome. He sows, but without knowing if

---

[38] As noted by St. John Climacus: "War against us is proof that we are making war" (*Ladder,* Step 4: "Obedience," p. 115).

he will reap, sometimes thoughts of fornication, sometimes thoughts of slander, and similarly for the other passions. He supplies nourishment to the passion which he sees the soul is slipping towards."[39]

Such Fathers understand the demons to engage with the natural arousal and concentration of the passions that occurs when man takes serious stock of his spiritual struggle; and, as such, that struggle is not simply against the interior impulses and appetites of the soul and body, but also against these foes who aggravate and accentuate those passions, seeking new ways to make man captive to dominating powers. Yet this is a desperate act: the demons, even the devil himself, do not attack with clear vision. Abba Matoes conveys that they simply attack willy-nilly, aggravating and sowing whatever passions they can, hoping one or another will take hold of the soul; and when they see that happening, they nourish that passion and feed it, so it may lead to others.

We see, in this, something of the coherence of the vision of the Fathers as to man's condition in this world. When man lives his life oriented toward the Kingdom, the passions take new hold in active ways; and the full character of the struggle man wages against these passions can only be understood when he also acknowledges the full, active reality of the demons. If he does not acknowledge the Kingdom and order his life according to it, man might never step out of the enslaving lethargy of worldly contentment. If he does not acknowledge the passions and understand them rightly as perversions of natural impulses which come to dominate and enslave, man can make no progress in identifying them rightly and accurately. And if he does not acknowledge the presence, reality, and activity of the demons, man cannot seriously work against the passions in himself, since

---

[39] Abba Matoes, Saying 4; in *The Sayings of the Desert Fathers: The Alphabetical Collection*, p. 143.

he will not know how they are being sown and strengthened, and whom he must oppose in order to defeat them.

It is for such reasons that the Christian today must work with renewed vigor to recapture in himself the right vision of these essential characteristics of the Life in Christ. The world opposes each of these quite directly: it does not acknowledge the Kingdom of God; it rejects even more potently the reality of demonic foes; and it has lost all sense of a proper distinction between natural impulse and dominating, passionate impulse—much less a concerted awareness of the true contours of the soul's fallen impulses and desires. At times it approximates a distinction between good habits and self-perceptions as opposed to bad, which seems to echo in some ways the Orthodox view of the passions; yet inasmuch as such distinctions aim to assist in discovering or creating a better self-definition, they continue to fall prey to the radical self-will of man and establishment of the self as the highest truth and greatest good—itself a passion identified by the Fathers.

The Christian attempting to live Christ's life in such a context, unless he overcomes the passions by adhering to the Church's authentic vision of such realities, works against himself. And so it is that in the modern day we must seek, as Christians of every age have had to seek, to approach the ascetical life in obedience to divine truth.

Relearning the Nature and Practice of Obedience

Let this mind be in you which was also in Christ Jesus, Who, being in the form of God, did not consider it robbery to be equal with God, but made Himself of no reputation, taking the form of a bondservant and coming in the likeness of men. And being found in appearance as a man, He humbled Himself and became obedient to the point of death, even the death of the Cross. Therefore God also has highly exalted Him and given Him the Name which is above every name, that at the Name of Jesus every knee should bow, of those in heaven, and of those on earth, and of those under the earth, and that every tongue should confess that Jesus Christ is Lord, to the glory of God the Father.[40]

Obedience responds to obedience. When someone obeys God, God obeys his request.

—Abba Mius of Belos[41]

Passion = complicary? "passivity"?

If man's passionate state is the fruit of rebellion, by which the natural but misdirected impulses come to dominate and captivate his heart, drawing it away from the remembrance of the Kingdom and further into the delusion of the demons, and if the ascetical struggle accentuates the passions, then a sure and safe guide through this struggle is necessary if man is to be saved from this sorry state and borne up into the life of the Holy Trinity. This way has been forged and offered by Jesus Christ, Whose incarnate life and offering of love at the Cross brought Him to the Resurrection, in which the power of the passions and the demons was overthrown. A newness of life was given to man. What remains is for man to receive it, to live it, and to bring to fruit in himself—by the activity of the Holy Spirit—that Life in Christ which conquers rebellion and death.

As the passions are perversions of natural impulses, particularly grounded in self-love and the disfigured appetite that seeks sensual pleasure, it is understandable that they have a distinct root. The Fathers identify this root as a singular perversion of will: that of arrogance, of pride. It is pride that first led Satan to rebel against God, causing him to envy man in Paradise and so tempt Adam and Eve. And though the first-created man is tempted into sin by this enemy, rather than arbitrarily seeking it

---

[40] Philippians 2:5–11.

[41] Abba Mius of Belos, Saying 1; in *The Sayings of the Desert Fathers: The Alphabetical Collection*, p. 150.

In my pride I saw everyone around me as complacent.

46

of his own accord, it is nonetheless the devil's playing on pride that allows the transgression: he instills and fosters pride in the hearts of the first parents, assuring them that they can "be like God."[42] The other passions which reign so freely over the human heart have their source here. And so it is that the Fathers also identify a chief virtue to combat this chief passion: namely, obedience, which engenders the humility that conquers pride.

Obedience—so misunderstood in our day as to be equated with a slavish mindlessness or occupation by another's whims— is at the very heart of the patristic vision of man's ascetical life. It is crucial that we come to understand it rightly, if we are to be armed properly with the tools the Church provides to advance in the spiritual contest.

Obedience is the virtue of a life in which self-will is sacrificed at the altar of the Cross, and the human person is united fully to the will of God. It is full communion in the life of Christ Himself, Who was *obedient unto death*. As such, obedience is the highest virtue; yet it is also the most basic and the most foundational for all spiritual endeavor. In the ascetical struggle, this heavenly obedience is wrought through living, practical obedience in this life, in which the will is voluntarily laid down before the will of the Church (which is Christ's will) through her doctrines, pastors, teachers, and spiritual fathers, so that the person may grow accustomed in himself to the obedience that unites him to the true Source of Life. It is thus a first step that enables all other steps in the spiritual struggle. As is written by St. Diadochus:

> It is well known that obedience is the chief among the initiatory virtues, for first it displaces presumption and then it engenders humility within us. Thus it becomes, for those who willingly embrace it, a door leading to the love of God. It was because he rejected humility that Adam fell into the lowest depths of hades. It was because He loved humility that the

---

[42] Cf. Genesis 3:5.

Lord, in accordance with the divine purpose, was obedient to His Father even to the Cross and death, although He was in no way inferior to the Father; and so through His own obedience He has freed mankind from the crime of disobedience and leads back to the blessedness of eternal life all who live in obedience. Thus humility should be the first concern of those who are fighting the presumption of the devil, for as we advance it will be a sure guide to all the paths of virtue.[43]

Here we see the direct linkage of pride to the devil, and the immediate relationship of obedience to the humility that overcomes it. Obedience is an "initiatory virtue" because it is one which sets the context for all other struggles of growth in Christ. Unless the heart comes to train its will to conform to Christ's, unless the fascination with "self" and with its desires and definitions gives way to the Lord's definition of His creature's life, man lives in a state of foundational separation from God. He ultimately is his own god, for his will is made his highest authority. His comforts define what actions or beliefs he will consider acceptable. His thoughts on truth and meaning define his reality.

This captivity to the will, in the mystery of sin's depth and extent, makes man into a kind of demon unto himself. Just as the soul can be angelic in function (though not in nature) when it emulates the angels in guiding the whole man toward God, so can it also emulate the work of the demons when it serves to guide him in the opposite direction.[44] In his essential ascetical text, *The Ladder of Divine Ascent,* St. John Climacus notes:

---

[43] St. Diadochus, *On Spiritual Knowledge,* 41, in the *Philokalia,* vol. 1, p. 265.

[44] On the soul, guided by the virtues, taking on an angelic function, see St. Maximus the Confessor, *Ad Thalassium* 17 (English translation in *St. Maximus the Confessor: On the Cosmic Mystery of Jesus Christ,* trans. Paul M. Blowers and Robert Louis Wilken [Crestwood, N.Y.: St. Vladimir's Seminary Press, 2003], pp. 107–8). In particular, St. Maximus identifies God's word (Holy Scripture), given in the divine precepts of virtue, coming thus as "an-

The proud monk needs no demon. He has turned into one, an enemy to himself.[45]

This stark observation serves as a warning to Christians in every age: where obedience does not form the will, the will shall form of itself an idol, and shall itself tyrannize man after the manner of the demons. If at times the demons seem remote, inactive in our lives, it is often because we have internalized their work through the passionate captivity of our lives. They have little to interject in order for their work to be accomplished.[46] Such insights reveal something of the true nature of obedience: it is not the slavish abandonment of the person by becoming drone-like in mimicking another, but the discovery of one's true created nature by entering into a living relationship—a relationship of love that draws the will out of its self-preoccupation, opening it up to communion in God's will. Obedience is a relationship, and thus active in nature (obedience as being dominated into "passivity" would itself be a form of *pathos*—a passion): and it is an active life in which self-will is *voluntarily abandoned* and one is joined to the will of another, by this practical measure softening the heart to receive the will of God and respond as if it were its own. This is the obedience imaged in the incarnate Lord, Who prayed to His Father: *Not My will, but Thine be done.*[47] Christ does not pray that His own will be replaced by another's; rather, He manifests the true state of

Handwritten margin note: We were in heaven then, up in the upper rooms or so we assumed.

---

gels" to man's struggle; the soul, following such precepts, takes on the angelic function of proclaiming God's presence and truth and guiding man aright. This must not, however, be confused for a claim that the soul becomes angelic by nature: St. Maximus speaks of function and activity, not being.

[45] *Ladder,* Step 23: "On Pride," p. 210. St. John elsewhere notes that "those beasts have another trick, of which I am aware; namely, to depart when the soul has become thoroughly imbued with the habits of evil, when it has turned into its own betrayer and enemy" (Step 26: "On Discernment," p. 238).

[46] See below, *A Century on Prayer and Watchfulness,* §15ff, p. 76ff.

[47] Luke 22:42. Cf. Matthew 26:39.

obedience as one in which the heart is wholly shaped by the divine will of the Father.[48]

True obedience is the full depth of a life offered to God. It is the willful offering, not simply of various aspects of our lives, our possessions, our thoughts to God, but the offering of our entire being, including our full heart and mind, to be wholly His and wholly defined by His creative energies. This is commented upon by St. Gregory the Great:

> By the other virtues, we offer God what we possess; but by obedience, we offer ourselves to Him. They who obey are conquerors, because by submitting themselves to obedience they triumph over the angels, who fell through disobedience.

In the words of St. Gregory, obedience is the offering of one's whole life to Christ—one's very being, rather than the circumstances and possessions of one's life. This is above all through the offering of the heart, which in the patristic vision is the locus of the mind and will: an offering which abandons the desire to define life and self by the working of the will, and which defines them instead by the divine will of the Creator.

The Church gives practical shape to this obedience in the ascetical life in numerous ways. Firstly, obedience is shaped and fostered through the right relationship of the Christian to the liturgical cycle of the divine services. The Church prescribes a life oriented to communion in the Mysteries through these services

---

[48] This is emphasized by St. Maximus in his *Opusculum* 6, where he notes that the phrase *not My will but Thine* indicates a "perfect harmony and concurrence," confirming "the ultimate concurrence of [Christ's] human will with the divine will, which is both His and the Father's; and ... that with the duality of His natures there are two wills and two operations respective to the two natures, and that He admits of no opposition between them, even though He maintains all the while the difference between the two natures from which, in which, and which He is by nature" (in *Cosmic Mystery,* trans. Blowers and Wilken, pp. 173–74).

and prayers—do we keep to that ordered life? Or do we shape our participation in the Church's liturgical cycle by our own desires and whims? Proper attendance at the regular weekly and festal services is a Christian's bare minimum of obedience to the worshipping life of the Church, which not only exposes him to the divine life present in those services and draws him up into the Kingdom, but also transforms his self-will through this small obedience.

Secondly, the Church fosters obedience through the Christian's adherence to her canons. This is not to say that all the faithful must have a deep knowledge of the canons (indeed, focusing too much on the letter of the canons proves spiritually harmful in a majority of circumstances, and it ought to be a more commonplace Orthodox pattern that collections of the canons, such as the *Rudder,* should only be read with a blessing); rather, it is to say that those canons *which directly bear on the life of all Christian persons* ought to be approached in a right spirit of obedience, rather than self-willed assessment. These are the canons that encourage Confession regularly, tied into Communion; that spell out practices in the temple such as physical posture and actions, as well as engagement in prayers and commemorations; the canons that give shape to fasting, and which define acceptable behaviors during fasting and other periods, both in and out of the church building. Too often we approach these as "guidelines" that we can assess for ourselves, taking from them what seems best for us; but this is not an approach of obedience that allows these canons any room to transfigure our heart. We must seek to encourage in ourselves a true spirit of obedience to the canons that bear upon us, which the Church gives to us (rather than those which we seek out on our own initiative), so that they become genuinely transformative tools in our ascetical growth.

Thirdly, the Church fosters obedience through the Christian's relationship to his or her spiritual father. Every Orthodox Christian has a spiritual father, for every Orthodox Christian, except those in the most rare of circumstances, has a priest—even if this priest is remote and not seen every day. Too often, we are driven by idealized portraits of what a "real" spiritual father ought to be, and so we fail to see the Church's provision in her pastors. This does not mean that every priest is a great beacon of spiritual wisdom: but every priest *is* imbued with the charism of the Holy Spirit, to guide his bishop's flock into right life through a relationship of obedience. And every Christian person is able to make the relationship he has with his priest (even if it not be terribly deep or inspiring) into an avenue of obedience. Even difficult pastoral relationships offer this possibility. What is essential is that we learn to lay down our wills before another; to accept pastoral counsel as something to be heeded, considering it in light of the teachings of the Gospels rather than our own whims and predilections. We must remember that even when we may seem to receive little spiritual instruction or insight, we are still provided with a valuable opportunity to crucify our self-will, laying it down even before the weakness of another, to the benefit and growth of our spiritual struggle.

Bearing a Better, Stronger Witness in the World

Have I not commanded thee? Be strong and of good courage; do not be afraid, nor be dismayed, for the Lord thy God is with thee wherever thou goest.[49]

The Christian struggle is waged in the heart, for this is the focal point of creation itself. It is here that we see the fullness of the Creator's purpose, and here that the whole of creation finds its summation. It is the human person who is the capstone of God's creative work, which exists as a microcosm of all creation. And so any struggle which seeks to Christianize the cosmos, to evangelize and fulfill Christ's call to mission, yet which does

---

[49] Joshua 1:9.

not begin with the human heart, works with secondary things rather than primary. Such action is analogous to one who seeks to repair a crumbling house by working on its outer timbers, while its foundations remain in crumbling disintegration. The foundations must be repaired and strengthened first; only then can the remainder of the structure be repaired in a manner that will last, that will abide.

So it is with the Christian life. Ascesis begins in the heart: in obediently reorienting the heart toward the Kingdom, in understanding its enemies and the passions that lay buried within it, and coming to combat and defeat them by Christ's power.

The Christian engages in this action, not as a selfish pursuit aimed solely at the benefit of his own person, but because he knows that *it is in the genuine ascesis of the heart that authentic Christian mission has its true foundation.* Without it, he scrambles to aid a broken world while broken himself; he tries to offer healing of an ailment of which he suffers most of all. He can only be truly of aid, of genuine witness, when he learns to cry out to Christ, "Thou hast come into the world to save sinners, *of whom I am chief,*"[50] and from that cry works to live a sober, serious, authentic Christian life of struggle and growth.

This realization of the ascetical nature of Christian mission serves a twofold purpose in our lives. Firstly, it reminds us that to fulfill the call to mission—which is the call of every Christian: none is exempt—we must take serious stock of our struggle and our lives, and work to better what is wanting. But secondly, it serves to remind us that it is precisely in our serious attentiveness to this struggle and its right contours, that we have the power to speak to the world the true message of Christ, of the Spirit, of the Father.

To live out Christian mission in the world requires of us a renewed boldness. It takes boldness to live authentically the Life in

---

50 Cf. I Timothy 1:15.

Christ in a world that not so much combats as ridicules it. It takes boldness to think, speak, act, and orient one's whole life toward a Kingdom, the very existence of which may be questioned by those around us. It takes boldness to acknowledge the reality of the demons and demonic power in a world where this will likely cause one to be branded simple, naïve, even crazy. It takes boldness to speak of the passions, especially in a world that more and more challenges definitions of "wrong" activities, negative impulses of the heart, etc. It takes boldness to seek obedience and proclaim its virtues in a world that understands it in debased terms.

Yet the moment we cease to live and proclaim these things, we cease to have any real potential as missionaries of the risen Christ. We become as *salt that has lost its flavor*.[51] We become evangelists without the *evangelion*; apostles with nothing to proclaim. And so the world, not to its discredit but to ours, takes the message we preach as but another philosophy, another option in a wide-ranging selection of belief systems. We dilute our witness, and so the world receives a diluted vision of the Faith that does not heal or satisfy, rather than the pure drink of which Christ says, *Whoever drinks of the water I shall give him will never thirst again*.[52]

Let this be, for us, a great call to action. Let us heed the warning given to St. John in his vision of the Apocalypse: *I would that thou wert hot or cold; but since thou art lukewarm, ... I will spit thee out of My mouth*.[53] We must rise up in genuine witness to the Life in Christ in all its authenticity—whatever the world may think of this; for by it, the world can be healed. It can be transformed, for this is what the Lord wills. Let us learn to live this life without adulteration, in its full scope, and bear witness in the world of this full life.

---

[51] Cf. Matthew 5:13; Mark 9:50; Luke 14:34.

[52] John 4:14.

[53] Apocalypse 3:15, 16.

The Transformative Power of the Attentive Heart

CHRIST CALLS the Christian to take stock of his condition daily. The contest of Christian life is waged every day, at every moment. When the contours of this contest are known, that daily assessment becomes a life-giving ascetical work, for it opens the heart to the true workings of the Giver of Life. So St. Basil can write:

> Examine what sort of being you are. Know your own nature, that your body is mortal but your soul is immortal, and that our life is twofold in kind. One kind is proper to the flesh, quickly passing by, while the other is akin to the soul, not admitting of circumscription. Therefore be attentive to yourself,[1] neither remaining in mortal things as if they were eternal, nor despising eternal things as if they were passing.... Understand yourself with all exactness, that you may know what gift to apportion to each—for the flesh nourishment and coverings, and for the soul doctrines of piety, education in courtesy, training in virtue, correction of the passions.[2]

By knowing the contours of one's life, sinful as it is, one can engage fully in the work of attaining the Kingdom through the defeat of the passions, overcoming the strength of the foe through the incomparable power of Jesus Christ. The life now lived can be offered more wholly to the Lord, Who will make our lives His own. Self-will can be gradually overcome, so that we begin more fully to live that reality of identity in Christ which

---

[1] Deuteronomy 15:9.
[2] St. Basil, *Homily on the Words "Be Attentive to Yourself,"* 3, pp. 96–97.

His own prayer proclaims: that we cry, "Our Father," as, by nature, only His Son can do. This is what it means for man to live *Life in Christ*. He is borne up in Christ's life, through union with Him made a child of the Father. The human person is made a son, a daughter, of the Lord. We are able to cry, "*Our* Father," because Christ leads us out of separation from God, away from a "self" defined by our will and passions, into a new life that is the work of His hands, the fruit of His will, the created glory of His eternal, unending and glorious life.

PART II

The Beginnings of a Life of Prayer

A view of the summit of Mount Athos, Greece, with the cross that
was erected there at the end of the nineteenth century.
Photograph from *Gora Afon: Gora Svyataya* (Mount Athos:
The Holy Mountain) (Moscow: Leto, 2002).

to believe
is to know

The Beginnings of Prayer

THE BEGINNINGS of prayer reside in the desire of the heart to know God.

Then, more than simply to know Him, the beginnings of prayer rise to the desire to abide and rest at every moment with Him Who showed His love upon the precious Cross.

The beginnings of prayer do not reside in a method, in a specific style or form of practice. They are a cry of the heart, a longing of the soul. If you have discovered this longing within yourself, even if its precise shape or source or focus remains unknown to you, then you have within you the seeds from which prayer can grow. But these seeds must be fostered, watered! The good seeds of growth into the Kingdom come one and all from the common source of our man-befriending God Himself; yet they fall on many kinds of soil—some of which foster growth, others death.[1] We must labor with active love to make of the soil of our heart a rich earth in which these beginnings of prayer may flower into the fullness of communion with God.

This will be a struggle and an act of ascetical labor, for in our day the "soil" into which the Word of God is cast is sadly deprived of nourishment and life. It is a soil that chokes out growth at every opportunity. The world today suffers from a sadly debased understanding of prayer—and this at a time when it is most in need of its true depths. Prayer limps along on the weak, feeble limbs of conversation, dialogue, and mere discourse with God. It has become a thing of words, mirroring worldly conver-

---

[1] Cf. Matthew 13:1–23.

sations on divine themes; but it is not that which might push the heart to the lofty heights of true communion in the Holy Trinity, which might bring man to the direct embrace of God Himself.

There is, however, a longing among many who cling to the Faith with pure hearts and a real desire, to go beyond these shallow waters of prayer to the very riches of divine communion promised in the Fathers, promised by Christ Himself.[2] This is the great hope of the present generation: that for all its dryness of faith, for all its lukewarm grasp of the evangelical life, for all its shy embrace of the true humility of the Cross, the longing for God has not left the heart of man. The creature still cries out for its Creator. In the shadow of the feeble, weak construct that the world is content to pass off as Christianity, the heart still longs for something more.

This desire, however, must be translated. It must become the fodder for real action. The longing for the ascent to true life is a necessary step in spiritual growth, yet without deeds it is only intention. The Life in Christ, however, is not a life of intention—it is a life of action. Christ turns to His would-be disciple who wishes to know the way to redemption, and says, *Come, take up the cross, and follow Me.*[3] He says in another place, *If thou wouldst be perfect, go, sell all thou hast ... and come follow Me.*[4] The intention to follow must give rise to the act of true following. The desire to be a Christian must be vivified by an embrace of the Saviour's Cross. The wish to attain the Kingdom must be given flight by an actual struggling forward along the "narrow path."[5]

And so it is with prayer. The beginnings of prayer reside in

mere intention

---

[2] Cf. John 17:20–21: *I do not pray for these alone, but also for those who will believe in Me through their word; that they all may be one, as Thou, Father, art in Me, and I in Thee; that they also may be one in Us, that the world may believe that Thou hast sent Me.*

[3] Mark 10:21.

[4] Matthew 19:21.

[5] Cf. Matthew 7:14; Luke 13:24.

the desire of the heart to know God, to rest with Him at every moment; but growth in prayer requires that we make out of this desire a life-changing course of action. It requires that we so order our lives that the heart *can* know God, and no longer be stripped of His glory and driven from His presence by our sin. It requires that we so shape our days that the heart *may* find rest in the Lord, whereas now it finds false rest and solace in so many other things.

The Life in Christ cannot be theoretical, nor can our prayer. We are called by Christ not to ponder possibilities and hopes, but to *take up* our *bed and walk!*[6] It is time for the Lord, and for us, to act.[7]

Our task, as the weak and the struggling among Orthodox Christians, must therefore be to take the beginnings of real prayer—that heartfelt desire to hold communion with God in the heart—and transform this into a life where such communion is not just a hope, not merely an idea, but a lived reality: where it becomes the substance of life itself. Then can the beginnings of prayer become the first steps toward its maturity. And know this first and foremost, above all else: God desires that you reside in Him, far more than even you desire this rest. No one longs for you to come to true communion with the merciful Lord more ardently than the Lord Himself! When we hear in the Gospel that *there is more joy in heaven over one repenting sinner* than over many others,[8] when we are reminded that the Lord has fashioned us and knows us by name,[9] let such things be our reminders that the Lord longs for our true abiding in Him, and calls us always upward to this life.

---

[6] John 5:8.

[7] Cf. the deacon's charge at opening of the Divine Liturgy: "It is time for the Lord to act: Master, give the blessing"; from Psalm 118:126: "It is time for the Lord to act."

[8] Luke 15:7.

[9] Cf. Isaiah 43:1.

Though the aim of prayer may be lofty and high, this does not mean it is unattainable—for what is impossible for men is possible with God.[10] The human creature is promised the Kingdom! You are called to the fullness of true prayer! Let your encouragement always be the living example of the Elder Joseph of Egypt, whose disciple, asking about the extent of the Christian life, was glorified with a vision of the elder transformed in light and fire, speaking to you as much as to him: "If only you would will it, you could become all flame."[11]

PRAYER: THE NATURAL LIFE OF MAN

This is the radiant life that is open to you, to each one of us, as a precious child of our redeeming God; for prayer is the highest, and also the truest, form of human existence. It is the authentic reality of our created life, if this life is but lived as God has fashioned and formed it.

Let your heart be clear on this point, for by misunderstanding many are led astray. In fostering the beginnings of prayer toward its ripe flowering, you do not seek the supernatural; you seek, rather, the truly natural. You seek the heart's true home. You seek the authentic proportions of your God-molded life. In striving for intimate communion with the Creator, you seek but to find that which He has offered from the first and which constitutes the very fabric of your life: for the Lord *breathed into man's nostrils the breath of life, and man became a living being.*[12] The intimacy of true prayer is the promise of creation itself. God's Spirit will yet be the vivifying power of our lives.

Do not seek or strive after "supernatural" things, much less

---

[10] Cf. Matthew 19:26; Mark 10:27; Luke 18:27.

[11] Cf. Abba Joseph of Panephysis, Saying 7; in *The Sayings of the Desert Fathers: The Alphabetical Collection*, p. 103.

[12] Genesis 2:7.

for supposed spiritual states or ecstatic experiences. These are
more the tools of our own self-deception than they are even of
the devil's craftiness. Instead, seek in prayer nothing more than
that which is the true handiwork of God's creative power: a heart
that bears in itself His divine life. This is what it means to be human, for this is how God fashioned man—not as a debased creature that must be overcome or added-to in order to experience
divine things, but as a creature whose very heart is the meeting
place of heaven and earth. Seek, then, for the heart to become
no more than that which God has created it to be; for Christ
became truly man, and so by becoming true men ourselves, we
grow closer to Him.

What Keeps Us from Prayer?

If the possibility of attaining union with the ineffable and
eternal God, of "being perfect," of "becoming all flame," seems
incomprehensible and foreign, strange and alien to our nature,
we must understand that this alienation has its source not in our
nature itself, but in the sinful abuse of our nature. It is we—not
God, not the world—who have made ourselves into finite and
limited beings, so broken and removed from God's grace.

God, for His part, has fashioned for humanity a nature so
at one with His divine nature that it can part seas, walk on the
waters, control the winds, heal the sick, raise the dead, even rise
from the grave; but we have taken this nature and made it into
something that dies even before its death, which has so alien-
ated itself from God that it fails to see Him at all—even comes
to question His very existence. Then—and here is our greatest
folly—we take the limited dimensions of this debased existence
and define them as "normal," "natural," since they are what we
come to know most intimately; and anything which goes beyond
them we define as "unnatural" or "supernatural" and thereby develop a suspicion even towards those things which God promises

are man's proper lot—to speak with Him, to converse with Him, to see Him, to partake of His power and His promises.

We can never foster the development of prayer if we do not come to understand the great folly of this embrace of our sin! It is our sin that has come to define our reality—not because sin is "real" (for sin is an act, possessing no substance, no real being, of its own), but because we have made of it such a familiar friend that we have lost all sight of the reality God has fashioned.[13] We start to speak of our "fallen nature" as if it were a thing of some real existence, and then we are quick to allow this debased vision to inform the whole of reality as we see and explain it. We begin with the damnable lament that union with the good God is not possible, and soon we deny that man is good at all. We begin by denying the possibility of the perfection of the soul, and soon we deny that the soul even exists. We fail to see God present in the cosmos of His design, and soon we are confessing that He did not design the cosmos. And so, because our sin defines our vision, man soon comes to the place where he denies God altogether—a feat long ago accomplished in this world.

Do not let this blindness to the truth cloud your spiritual vision and keep you from the beginnings, much less the heights, of prayer! Remember that, for all his baseness, man is yet precious enough that the Father would send His only Son to sanctify and redeem him. Remember that you have been fashioned, not for some ignoble end, but for the glory of your Maker. Remember

---

[13] Cf. the words of St. Diadochus of Photiki (fifth century A.D.): "Evil does not exist by nature, nor is any man naturally evil, for God made nothing that was not good. When in the desire of his heart someone conceives and gives form to what in reality has no existence, then what he desires begins to exist. We should therefore turn our attention away from the inclination to evil and concentrate it on the remembrance of God; for good, which exists by nature, is more powerful than our inclination to evil. The one has existence while the other does not, except when we give it existence through our actions" (St. Diadochus, *On Spiritual Knowledge*, 3; in the *Philokalia,* vol. 1, p. 253).

that, despite all the power and potency of sin, there is yet nothing in all creation that is *able to separate us from the love of God that is in Christ Jesus our Lord.*[14]

Our sin limits our vision and perception, this is true; but the Lord came to give sight to the blind. The eyes of prayer can be opened. That noble and holy beginning, that desire of your heart, cannot be hindered or thwarted—not by sin, not by evil, not even by death—unless you will it so to be. But if we will instead that the gift of prayer, which our merciful God lovingly offers to all the world, be received and embraced, then all that hinders us from true rest in Christ will be stripped of its power, and the heart will live in the love of its Maker.

GOD HAS GIVEN PRAYER TO MAN AS A GIFT

Prayer may require our work, our effort (we must remember always that the Kingdom of God belongs to those who *take it by force*[15]), yet it is fundamentally a gift of God. A gift—freely given and lovingly bestowed.

No human effort or labor could ever unite creation and Creator, the made and the Maker, were it not infused with power by God's own grace. No ascesis or struggle could attain the high aim of receiving divine life, were it not blessed and bestowed by the Giver of Life Himself. The substance of true prayer, the union of the heart with God, is simply an impossibility for any created power, unless that power is given force by the love of God, drawn from Him and offered as a gift to the creature He longs to bring fully into life.

Dwell on what it means, then, for prayer to come to man as a gift of God's love. He gives man an aim, and the means to attain it. He supplies a charge given to no other creature in all

---

14 Romans 8:39.
15 Matthew 11:12.

the vast array of His creative works: to dwell, body and soul, in the fullness of His presence. Even the holy angels are not called to such a communion. The Lord gives this gift to man, not as an afterthought of creation, but as the very substance of man's life. *Human life is to be a life of prayer.* Man is to receive into his heart the "light of the world."[16] God and man are to live together, now and for all eternity.[17]

Behold how the whole divine economy—the history of our race in God's creation—has been shaped by this very gift. God fashioned man from the first for union with Himself. When the simplicity of divine communion was broken by transgression, when man welcomed into his heart another law and another love, God responded by preparing man for the return to His true grace. He Who was *slain from the foundation of the world*[18] prevented man from making his sin eternal by placing him outside of Paradise, that by toils and struggles he might find the way to the Cross, which mystically had been already present in the Garden.[19] When the time had fully come, He Himself entered into the world as man, as the new Adam, reuniting in Himself that which had become broken and divided in us, restoring to us the possibility for that union which true prayer represents. Sacrificing Himself upon the Cross, He

---

[16] Cf. John 1:9.

[17] Cf. the opening line of St. Innocent of Alaska's *Indication of the Way into the Kingdom of Heaven:* "People were created not only to live here on earth, like the animals, which disappear after their death; but with the sole purpose of living with God, and living not for a hundred or a thousand years, but eternally."

[18] Apocalypse 13:8. Cf. I Peter 1:18–20; I Corinthians 2:7–10.

[19] Cf. Genesis, chaps. 2–3, on the first transgression and the expulsion of Adam and Eve from Paradise. On the Tree of Life in Paradise as a prefiguration of the Cross, see p. 123, note 8 below. Many patristic writings and Church hymns also compare and contrast the Tree of Knowledge in Eden with the Cross; see Fr. Seraphim Rose, *Genesis, Creation, and Early Man,* 2nd edition (Platina, Calif.: St. Herman of Alaska Brotherhood, 2011), pp. 249, 277–82, 775.

underwent even death on our behalf, that the fruit of our sin might be overcome and defeated; and rising from the tomb, He "restored to life those who were fallen away."[20] The life promised in Eden—a life of glory and communion with God—was again presented to man. Ascending bodily into heaven, our Lord wrought fully in Himself all that is promised to us, and sent to us the Holy Spirit that our hearts might be stirred to His glory. So we are enabled to sing, "we have seen the resurrection of Christ,"[21] and with it we have seen the full promise of prayer and life bestowed so mercifully by God.

The beginnings of prayer, then, are the firstfruits in the heart of our truest longing, of our right and proper place in creation, of our blessed and true embrace of history, life, love, and divine calling. They are the heart's response to this gift God has bestowed from the first moments of creation, now realized not generically, as relating to the whole of creation, but in the life of this unique person whom God has fashioned.

It Is Time to Make a Beginning

When the heart comes to realize that the gifts God offers for the life of the whole world He also offers uniquely to each person, whom He loves with an immeasurable love and knows with an ineffable intimacy, these beginnings of prayer start to blossom. But their blossoming is not the end of our receipt of God's grace: it is still the beginning! Recognizing this cry of the heart, it is time to act—to make a start.

The beginnings of prayer must lead us to the attainment of prayer's truer substance. The power of God is not one merely to bless our spiritual infirmity, but to raise us up out of our illness. While not all ailments of the body may be healed in this

---

[20] Cf. the Theotokion of the Evlogitaria at Matins.
[21] Cf. the resurrectional troparion following the Gospel, at Matins.

life (for at times God grants blessed suffering, according to His mercy), the healing of soul is promised to every man; and so our task is to foster *growth* in prayer, that we may enter more fully into the promises of God. And let there be no thought or excuse that our spiritual infirmity is too great, that we are condemned to live only among weak reflections of prayer and communion with the Lord. Remember the story of the Lord's friend Lazarus, who was not only ill but in fact wholly dead, and that for four days.[22] Is your spiritual state more dire than his? But the Lord spoke a command to the dead man: *Lazarus, come forth!*—and the dead man arose. Likewise, He said to the dead daughter of Jairus: *Damsel, I say unto thee, arise!*—and the girl arose, and walked.[23]

The Lord calls out to each of us, also: "My child, arise! Get up from your slumber in sin and follow Me. Rise up from the palsy of your spiritual illness and walk in the fullness of the life I have come down from heaven to grant you. Receive from Me that which neither evil, nor sin, nor Satan, nor death could prevent Me from giving you: the heavenly life of My Kingdom!" And what are we to do when the Lord thus comes to us? Are we to remain stagnant and still? Or are we to turn to Him Who has revealed Himself to us and cry out with St. Thomas, *My Lord and my God!*[24]—and then rise up and follow Him?

It is time to make a beginning in prayer! There is no other time that God has given to man. How long shall we make excuses and so prevent our growth? Not for one more day, or even another moment. *Today, salvation is come into this house!*[25] Today is the day when our truer prayer may begin.

---

[22] See John 11:1–44.
[23] Mark 5:41–42.
[24] John 20:28.
[25] Luke 19:9.

The Need to Make a Realistic Beginning

If, however, we are to make a fruitful beginning, we must make a realistic beginning.[26] Our aim may be lofty and all creation may bear testimony to the reality we seek to approach; but we are weak creatures. We must never forget that we are frail and sinful, hardly worthy of the task of prayer, for if we forget this we will at once grow conceited and think of ourselves far more highly than we ought. But at the same time we must not allow our weakness, when seen in comparison with the exalted heights of prayer set before us, to cause us to grow despondent. God calls us to nothing less than perfect communion with Himself; but in His tenderness and wisdom He knows that the one whom He calls is crippled by sin, stuck fast in his error, barely able to move. And so the Lord provides for us to begin to pray, not with the great exaltations of light and fire and illumination, but with small and realistic steps that will lead us from our present condition to the life that awaits the children of God in His Kingdom.

When we seek to foster the beginnings of prayer into something more, we must keep our eyes realistically focused on our true spiritual state. It does no good for a man with severe injuries to his legs to pretend he is able to walk. In the same way, it does little good for a man who is severely spiritually injured by his sin and feeble life in the virtues to pretend he can pray at the heights of prayer's peak. We, each of us, must start with our true state. We must look to the examples of those who spoke with God face-to-face,[27] on whom God's light descended in a bright ray,[28]

---

[26] See below, *A Century on Prayer and Watchfulness,* §§78–84; pp. 90–91.

[27] E.g., Moses the God-Seer; see Exodus 33:11. See also Jacob in Genesis 32:30 as one who has "seen God face-to-face."

[28] E.g., St. Anthony the Great of Egypt; see St. Athanasius the Great, *Life of St. Anthony* 10, in *Athanasius: The Life of Antony and the Letter to Marcellinus,* trans. Robert C. Gregg (New York: Paulist Press, 1979), p. 39.

who became all flame,[29] who beheld the divine vision of God's uncreated glory;[30] but we must recognize that their light shines on us who are weak, helpless, blind, fallen, dark of soul, and enslaved by our sin. We cannot, must not, presume to pray in our state in the same way as they!

Rather, God will bless the small measures we take to respond to our spiritual condition, employing the steps toward prayer exemplified in the saints. God calls each of us, as we are, to become more than we are. Whatever our lot, we can grow in prayer. There are counsels in the Scriptures and the Fathers that can help us take practical steps to grow in Christ, by the power of His Spirit, to the glory of the heavenly Father.

DRAWING OUT PRACTICAL GUIDANCE FROM OUR ORTHODOX HERITAGE

Let us then turn to the practical guidance of the Fathers and the Scriptures, together with the worshipping life of the Church. Let us follow the pattern of those before us and draw out from their teachings those things which may be of encouragement to us who seek to make a good beginning today. In our generation, when our spiritual attention is so much diminished from that of previous ages, long tomes on prayer may easily overwhelm both mind and heart. We are like babes that cannot yet digest such solid and hearty food. We need forms of this spiritual food that are more easily digestible to our weak souls, that will call us to action—that will help us to see what is offered to us, how it is offered, and how we are to take it up and act.

In all things, let us strive to keep away from anything "new"

---

[29] E.g., Abba Joseph of Panephysis; see above, p. 62.

[30] E.g., St. Symeon the New Theologian; see *Ethical Discourses* 1.12, in *St. Symeon the New Theologian: On the Mystical Life,* vol. 1, trans. Alexander Golitzin (Crestwood, N.Y.: St. Vladimir's Seminary Press, 1995), pp. 77–78.

or "creative" in the realm of prayer and the spiritual life. Part of the problem with our spiritual condition today is the constant desire to invent and create a "spirituality" that will satisfy our wants and desires. Yet "to create" Christianity for ourselves is always to destroy Christianity; or more accurately, since the Church cannot be thwarted, it is to destroy in ourselves any real embrace of the Truth that God has shone into the world. The Life in Christ has, from the first, been a life *received:* a life handed to the Apostles by the Lord Himself, which they received and in due course handed on—and which even today we receive in this unbroken communion in truth and life. We do not seek "new" words on prayer; rather, we seek words that faithfully convey what the Church has always taught about prayer and its attainment—what is handed down to us in the Scriptures, the writings of the Holy Fathers, and the ascetical practices of Orthodox life.

A Note on the Centuries on Prayer

The two Centuries on Prayer which follow have been composed in the style of an old written genre found in the Fathers, namely the "century," or collection of one hundred short reflections. This form is particularly found among some of the early writers addressing topics of ascesis and prayer, given that the brief nature of the texts, instead of long segments of sustained narrative, allow reflections to be received at a pace that fosters contemplation rather than "study."

It is in gratitude to those Fathers whose words coming to us in such a form have always touched my own heart, that I have sought to take up that genre here. In this volume, each Century's main sections contain seven texts, in honor of the symphony of creation and the rest of the Lord on the seventh day. Within each of these, there are three groupings of two related texts, honoring the Holy Trinity and the incarnate Lord Jesus Christ in His two natures—divine and human—followed by a summary paragraph.

A Century on Prayer and Watchfulness

PRAYER AS SABBATH AND REST

1. Prayer is the call of God to the heart, and the response of the heart to God. It is the rest of which the Saviour spoke: *Take My yoke upon you and learn from Me, for I am gentle and lowly in heart, and you will find rest for your souls.*[1] It is the rest in which the soul and body, which *labor and are heavy laden*[2] by the burdens of this world, abide in the true Sabbath, in the comforting bosom of the Lord.

complacency

2. This rest is not one of idleness or absence; it is, rather, the rest of the Saviour Himself, Who in His ineffable condescension rested in the tomb on the Great and Most Holy Sabbath, drawing the departed back to life. The inner Sabbath of true prayer is the stillness of the heart in its Creator. There the Psalmist's words are obeyed: *Be still, and know that I am God,*[3] and the mystical resurrection of the ailing creature is begun in the depths of the heart.

3. As the Lord's rest creates life and His descent into hades proved the universal power of His Resurrection, so prayer is full of life in its stillness, and abundant in its rest, and it raises up the fallen in us by its divine power.

4. Just as the Saviour raised up Adam with Himself in the fulfillment of His mystical Sabbath on the seventh day, so too

---

[1] Matthew 11:29.
[2] Matthew 11:28.
[3] Psalm 45:11. Psalms are referenced throughout according to the Septuagint numbering and versification.

our heart, finding its rest in the Sabbath of prayer, will seek out the lost portions of our life and lift them up to our Master. And just as on the Great Sabbath Christ led all things to new life, so through the Sabbath of prayer the Spirit will lead us to communion in unending and undying life.

5. Like the gracious Saviour in the tomb, true prayer exists where a death to the world has already occurred. As long as the attractions and compulsions of worldly cares continue to bind the heart to the fruit of sin, the heart cannot find the rest in which its genuine longing is fulfilled.

6. The Resurrection came only after the tomb. So, too, the heights of prayer come only with our death to sin. We must entomb ourselves in the grave of repentance, remaining attached to no worldly thing, if we are to be lifted out of death to the life of prayerful communion in Christ.

7. So let us heed the angelic words of the earthly choirs who sing at the mystical Entrance, "Now let us lay aside all worldly cares, that we may receive the King of all."[4] For if we do not cast off such cares, do not die to them and flee from them as the waste of our former sin, we shall not find the stillness of heart necessary to receive the King; and it is the King Himself Who builds the edifice of true prayer within us, just as the Psalmist says: *Lift up your heads, O ye gates! And be lifted up, ye everlasting doors! And the King of glory shall enter in.*[5]

Combatting the Passions

8. How shall we cast off these binding cares? How shall we join our precious Saviour in the tomb? How shall we attain the mystical Sabbath in which we find the rest of prayer and contemplation? We shall make no progress in these things if we do not,

---

4 From the Cherubic Hymn of the Divine Liturgy of St. John Chrysostom.

5 Psalm 23:7.

first of all, discover the passions that war in us and set ourselves against them by the grace of ascetical warfare handed to us by our guardian mother, the holy Church of the Lord Himself.

9. To grow in prayer, then, we must be attentive to this rooting out of the passions. It is no good to say, "I shall pray," if we continue to give the passions free reign over the heart and mind. If we are to make a real beginning, we must make an intelligent one, as the Church directs. Else we are like the ailing man who says, "I shall now be well," but refuses to take the medicine prescribed by his doctor. It is foolishness, and a sign of our own pride.

10. The passions are the true enemies of prayer. Satan may oppose prayer, the demons may fight it; but the passions destroy the very space in the heart where prayer may grow. They prevent the edifice of prayer from ever being built. Their context can be compared to the building of a house: Satan is like one who terrifies the builders, so that they are afraid to engage in their task. The demons are like those who steal in by night and remove this plank or that, frustrating the efforts of the workers. But the passions are like a mold that has eaten its way into the foundation stones, weakening them into dust. Whatever is laid upon such foundations will inevitably fall.

11. If we wish to pray, then, let us begin by combatting anger, defeating lust, and destroying pride.

12. If, when we are combatting our fallen passions in the struggle for prayer, they are redoubled in their power, let us take heart. As the Fathers teach, the passions are concentrated in the heart that seeks the Lord; and the closer we draw to true contemplation, the more their force is focused against us.

13. As we see in the holy icon of the Ladder, the ascent of prayer calls the struggle against the passions into ever sharper relief. The higher we ascend, the more the passions draw together within us, for we become distanced from the worldly attractions and habits in which they are normally dispersed. This is why

some of our holiest and most God-bearing Fathers have experienced the struggle against the passions to so high a degree, while most of us are deadened to their presence and foolishly believe them to be minor things.

14. We cannot pray truly when we are dominated by the passions, for true prayer is the heart's rest in God, while the passions are the heart's captivity to its impulses and fallen desires. *You cannot serve* both *God and mammon;*[6] and if "mammon" represents, in earthly terms, our attachment to wealth and money, then in the spiritual life it represents our attachment to the compulsions of the passionate soul and body. If we wish to serve the man-befriending Lord and find our rest in Him, we must learn to serve Him alone and cast off the familiar masters that are our passions.

The Demons

15. The demons provoke and stir up the passions in a man who seeks authentic prayer, for they see in that one a man who actively works against their aims. Such a man has lifted himself out of the usual lethargy by which the demons' work is accomplished by man himself, without the requirement of their constant provocation; and to such a man they rush with renewed vigor. So we must not be surprised when, in those moments when we set our heart to true prayer, the demons collude against us with stronger force: this is neither arbitrary nor accidental. They act according to their true nature when, by God's love and grace, we begin to act according to ours.

16. The true terror of a demon is a man genuinely struggling after prayer. In the face of this threat, the demon will do everything in its power to upset its enemy: the Godly soul seeking sanctification.

17. Nevertheless, the demons' power is no power. They ex-

---

6 Matthew 6:24; Luke 16:13.

ercise force through deception and wield a sword through a lie. This is why our Holy Fathers instruct us that their defeat is so easy. By the simple sign of the precious Cross, the demons and all their terror can be put to flight.

18. The demons follow their chief, Satan, who *is a liar and the father of it.*[7] They convince the soul that they can foretell the future, when in truth they have power only to guess, or to behold with higher vision as spirits; they convince the soul that they have power to grant life and gifts, when they possess in reality only what they steal. What the soul ought to fear is not the demons' power in these regards, but rather their ability to deceive; for it is a deceived heart that remains at odds with its Lord.

19. By deception, the demons provoke the passions. The real defeat of man comes from within, not without. The demons provoke, but the passions corrupt. So let us exercise an awareness of demonic activity, but let us cast the deepest accusations against ourselves, where the passions are given reign to conquer our hearts.

20. We must remember that the demons could have no foothold in our hearts if our impurities did not prepare there an abode fitting to their presence. They reside where it is comfortable for them to live. So if we wish to attain to prayer unaffected by demonic temptation, let us begin by fostering purity of body and mind, that our house may become barren and uninviting to the demons and a fitting temple for the presence of the Lord.

21. All my passions rage against me at every hour, and the host of demons tempts me at every moment. Behold, the true state of my miserable soul! But the Lord looks into the heart of man and sees the trouble there, and He speaks the word that quiets the demons and calms the raging passions. Just as the Psalmist declares, *My help cometh from the Lord, Who hath made*

---

[7] John 8:44.

[handwritten note: not "the devil and God are raging inside me, but the devil, and God is the peacemaker]

heaven and earth,[8] so must we remember that true prayer comes ever from this gracious Lord, Who defeats the enemies that war against us.

DEFEATING THE PASSIONS IN PRAYER

22. If we wage war against the passions by a consistent repentance and gentle obedience, the purification provided by the grace of the Holy Trinity will become our ally and aid in their defeat. Just as misguided passions prevent the heart from fully approaching union with God, repelling its every impulse to communion in the splendor of the Lord, so a mind devoutly intent on inner prayer naturally repels those passions which fail to drive the soul closer to Christ. In this way, the aim of our contest also becomes the tool of its attainment.

23. When a mind is focused on true prayer, its desires for earthly passions are weakened by its longing for divine union. The truer longing displaces its weak, disfigured brother. Seen in a renewed way as obstacles to pure prayer, familiar passions such as anger, greed, and lust are driven out, that the mind might be clear and holy, made ready for spiritual contemplation.

24. Look, how visible is God's mercy! In His infinite love He makes prayer the very tool by which we may learn to pray! He gives us prayer, which weakens the passions that keep us from prayer, so that by what is at first a weak and surface-level contemplation we might mature in due course to the heights of divine communion. How little ought we to fear the obstacles that lie in our way, in the face of such love and divine favor from the Lord!

25. There are times when, in His infinite loving-kindness, the tender Lord banishes the passionate impulses wholly from our hearts for a brief time in prayer. This wonderful solace serves

---

[8] Psalm 120:2.

to show us what can be obtained through genuine repentance, giving us a foretaste of blessed dispassion. If ever this miracle is wrought in us, let us embrace it not as a sign of our maturity or accomplishment; rather, let us recognize it as a condescension to our great sin: that the Lord provides us, even in our unworthiness, with a glimpse of Paradise. And so let us rise up with new vigor to its right and full attainment.

26. Gentleness of heart is a tool of infinite value in the struggle against the passions. Just as the king declared to the Lord, *Thy gentleness hath made me great,*[9] so too the gentleness of the Lord's presence may distill the troubles of the heart and raise us to the great heights of prayer. But we will not find gentleness where our will reigns, for an unchecked will is the father of arrogance and pomposity. The Lord's gentleness, however, comes to us through humility and obedience.

27. The Lord Himself is our example in this: in all things was He obedient to His Father, even saying to His disciples, *I have come down from heaven not to do Mine own will, but the will of Him Who sent Me,*[10] and in the garden, *Not My will, but Thine be done.*[11] So was He *gentle and lowly in heart,*[12] One Who *humbled Himself,*[13] Who *opened not His mouth,*[14] Who was kind to the sinner even as He pronounced the just and mysterious judgment of the Kingdom. In this, the Saviour was ever in perfect communion with His Father and the Holy Spirit, for the gentleness of His obediently humble will maintained at all times that divine union, untouched by the passions that might thwart it.

28. If we are to discover true prayer, let the passions be ban-

---

9 II Kingdoms 22:36.
10 John 6:38.
11 Luke 22:42.
12 Matthew 11:29.
13 Philippians 2:8.
14 Acts 8:32; Isaiah 53:7. Cf. Psalm 38:10.

ished through our intent and our unbending love of the Lord. We cannot pray if we do not conform our will to His; and we cannot emulate the Lord's will if ours is held captive by the passions. Let us cast off this heavy yoke of sin, and take upon us instead the yoke of the Saviour, which is light and easy to bear.[15]

ANGER, THE OPPONENT OF PRAYER

29. As the Holy Fathers teach us, prayer itself can be directed against the passions that disrupt the heart. If we find that we are angry with one person or another when we strive to pray, let us direct our prayer against that passion by praying for the person against whom we have sinned. If we are worried for this one or that, let us remember him especially in our prayer. In this way, prayer calms the passions that prevent the deeper contemplation of God.

30. Different passions will disrupt the heart in different ways, and so pose different obstacles to prayer. For the more physical, sensual passions, fasting and ascetical labors will often prove a useful aid, and to some extent may free the mind from them in prayer. But the more a passion is centered in the heart, the more it works its way into the very temple of prayer itself, defiling it. This is particularly the case with the more emotive passions such as lust and, above all, anger.

31. Anger against our brother is a poison to prayer—a poison more potent than almost any other. If, when we pray, we discover such an anger in our heart, we must combat it immediately; else, we mix the poison into the draught we drink, and a small ailment becomes immeasurably greater.

32. Anger is a fuel for all the passions and a provocation of the demons. Let us remember the life of our holy Father Isidore of Scetis who, when asked why the demons were so terrified of

---

[15] Cf. Matthew 11:30.

him, replied, "Ever since I became a monk I have tried never to let anger rise as far as my mouth."[16]

33. I have been instructed that the surest route to conquering anger against a brother in prayer is to seek his salvation and mine together with an abundance of prostrations. When we recognize such an anger in ourselves, let us first remember that it is we who are sinners, not our brother, and that anger is a sign of our own weakness. Then let us fall prostrate and beg the loving Lord: "My Creator, save me through the prayers of my brother!" If we do this a hundred times, the Lord will calm the passions of our heart.

34. If our anger remains after one hundred prostrations, by all means let us perform another hundred. And then another, if it be needed. And if we must keep from sleep through the whole night and prostrate ourselves to the rising of the sun for the sake of defeating the anger we harbor against our brother, so be it! It is better to cast off sleep than to lose our souls.

35. Only let us never imagine that we can offer true prayer in the temple of our souls and bodies while they rage with anger against our brother. We are then convicted by the words of St. John: *If we say that we have no sin, we deceive ourselves, and the truth is not in us.*[17]

Struggles in Prayer; Seeking Comfort in Prayer

36. The best solace for a troubled mind is the practice of prayer, for through prayer the mind is purged of worry and distress, and these are replaced with the refreshing light of Christ within the soul.

37. We will not always feel this solace when we pray: indeed,

---

[16] Cf. *The Sayings of the Desert Fathers: The Alphabetical Collection*, pp. 96–97.

[17] I John 1:8.

there are times when, due to the hardness of our hearts, our prayer will serve to show up our lack of dispassion and make it painfully obvious to our minds. It is then that we cry out to the Lord: *The waters have surrounded me, even to my soul; the deep has closed in around me.*[18] It is then that prayer does not seem to ease the heart but causes us to cry out with greater conviction: *I am weighed down by many an iron fetter, I am rejected because of my sins, and I have no relief.*[19] Yet in these moments we must not despair: the Lord in His tender mercy knows our heart and our struggle, and, when it is most fitting for our salvation, He allows prayer to convict rather than ease our minds. In this we are provided with a precious opportunity to be humbled by our sin.

38. True prayer is a function of the heart, and if we were genuinely attentive to preserving the stillness of the heart in the Lord, our prayer would not be tossed to and fro by the affairs of the external world. Yet our sin draws us out of the heart, and there arise situations that prevent, or at least make difficult, a true devotion in prayer. The result is a feeling of emptiness, or at times a kind of dryness: symptoms that suggest a removal from God. But in these moments it is yet best to pray, for even by means of a shallow and unfocused prayer the lips still call upon the Name of Christ; and where the lips lead, the heart will follow.

39. I have sometimes found that my heart is cold when I pray, yet through the acts and words of prayer is warmed by Christ. But I have never found that my cold heart is warmed without it.

40. The greater the coldness of heart and inattentiveness of the mind in prayer, the more we ought to rely on the helpmeet of prostrations. The holy Apostle tells us that *at the Name of Jesus every knee shall bow:*[20] let us, then, bow the knees of our bodies when our heart finds it difficult to call out this Name!

---

[18] Jonah 2:6.
[19] Prayer of Manasseh, v. 10.
[20] Philippians 2:10.

41. If, when we are seated at prayer, our mind wanders, let us stand. If words said in silence are overpowered by a distracted mind, let us speak them aloud. If, in standing, our minds continue to go astray, let us fall down again and again on our faces in our prayer. The body may at times oppose us, but it can also be our helpmeet and tool. Let us not forget to use the body to call our heart and mind to task.

42. Make the sign of the precious Cross when you pray. Without it, you will never find the joy of true prayer; for "through the Cross, joy has come into all the world."[21]

PRAYER AND MYSTERY; THE RATIONAL MIND

43. Prayer is a mystery. It can be attained only in a mystery.

44. We must never forget this essential mystery at the heart of prayer! We must never let our weakened minds see prayer as simply a conversation, as a mere exchange of words. These are the tools of prayer at certain levels; but the depth of prayer is the quiet rest of the heart in loving communion with its Maker.

45. Prayer is the union of a finite being with God, Whose nature is infinite and Whose existence is eternal. By it, the substance of the former is made holy, and the image of the latter is made more clearly manifest in the human race.

46. When we are told that "if you pray truly, you are a theologian,"[22] we are reminded of both the majesty of prayer and the true nature of theology. Our salvation is not to be found in books or letters: it consists in the communion of the heart in God. Let us attain this theology through repentance!

---

[21] From the hymn at Sunday Matins, "Having beheld the Resurrection of Christ."

[22] Evagrius of Pontus, *On Prayer: One Hundred and Fifty-Three Texts,* 61; in the *Philokalia,* vol. 1, p. 62.

47. Prayer is the cure for a diseased mind. The intellect that believes it can gain the Kingdom by rational power has only this cure—that is, prayer—as sufficient for its ailment.

48. In our modern age, where the mystery of God is ever more thoroughly removed from man's vision through a growing faith in debased rationalism, this remedy is difficult for some to prescribe, more difficult still for most to swallow. Yet it has the power to transform the dead bones of debased reason into the living assembly of divine and true knowledge.[23]

49. Prayer is not the antithesis of reason: it is an activity of the heart and mind beyond reason. It does not deny the intellect: it perfects and transcends it. Prayer does not say to modern man, "Deny your rational faculty," for this too is the gift of God. Rather, prayer says, "Remember that your reason is like a foundation stone. It is good and can be pure; but unless something is built upon it, its existence is in vain."

PRAYER IN THE HOLY SPIRIT

50. The beginnings of prayer reside in a simple phrase: "Lord, have mercy," but the heights of prayer go beyond all words. The holy Apostle Paul reveals this when he affirms that the Holy Spirit *Himself makes intercession for us.*[24] For, as the Saint says, the Spirit dwells in you;[25] and so He manifests prayer in our innermost being, where our own words are incapable of expressing the true groanings of the heart.

51. When we are weak in prayer, when we are ailing in spirit and broken in body, then let us fall upon the Lord's promise with deeper conviction. It is then that the Spirit shall bind our wounds, touch our hearts, and lift up our prayer to the Father.

52. We must endeavor not to do battle with the Spirit, Who

---

[23] Cf. Ezekiel 37:1–14.
[24] Romans 8:26.
[25] Cf. Romans 8:11.

is our Helper and Comforter in prayer. We do battle with Him when we defile His dwelling-place, our body, with lustful passions; and we do battle with Him when we muffle His divine voice with our paltry words. Let us offer instead a pure body and a quiet heart, for these present the Spirit with a peaceful country in which to reign.

53. Fall upon prayer as your only aid and help in this life. When you are weary, pray. When you are joyful, let your joy feed deeper prayer. When in hunger or thirst, open your heart to the Lord. When in exultation, bind your life more firmly to God. When prayer itself is hard, pray all the more. For prayer is "the ascent of the heart to God,"[26] Who is its true and proper Master in every condition of this life.

54. This Spirit knows your heart better than you do. When through weariness or inattentiveness you fall dumb in prayerful openness before the Lord, do not fancifully invent conditions to present to the Master. Quiet your mind, and let the Spirit reveal the true condition of your heart.

55. To pray without the Spirit is to breathe without air, or eat without food, or drink without water. It is impossible: yet how often we make the vain attempt!

56. When the Spirit prays in a man, his heart is transformed from a cold rock to a living fire. The unsatisfying water of his soul becomes the true wine of spiritual life.[27] The raging sea of his mind is parted, that he might come directly into the presence of his Lord.[28] The meager rations of his Christian life are multiplied a hundredfold into the nourishment of the eternal Kingdom.[29] In short, all the miracles of God's love are manifested in the heart where the Spirit has kindled the flame of true prayer.

---

[26] Cf. Evagrius of Pontus, *On Prayer,* 36; in the *Philokalia,* vol. 1, p. 60.

[27] Cf. John 2:1–11.

[28] Cf. Exodus 14.

[29] Cf. Matthew 14:13–21, 15:32–38; Mark 6:30–44; Luke 9:10–17; John 6:1–14.

THE RELATIONSHIP OF REPENTANCE TO PRAYER

57. If we wish to pray in the Spirit, but make no attempt to purify ourselves through ascesis, can we expect any fruits for our labors? Can we expect to welcome Him into a temple to which we have barred up all the doors through our passions? Ought we to expect Him to sit upon a throne we continue to muddy with our sins? So we must begin the ascent of prayer with purification, that prayer's Master might be with us.

58. The beginnings of such ascesis lie in repentance, which turns the heart from sin to true life. Repentance and prayer are inseparable kinsmen. The one will not be found without the other.

59. I have tried many times to pray, but have found my prayer to be lifeless and dry because I approached it with an unrepentant heart. Prayer was then my production, my construction, my false edifice; and like the tower at Shinar before it, the Lord in His mercy destroyed my vain attempt to gain the Kingdom through arrogance and pride.[30]

60. Where arrogance and pride lead, prayer does not follow. Oil and water may appear to mix together for a time, but eventually the one will repulse the other. So prayer may appear to exist in an unrepentant heart that is the haven of pride and the other passions; but in due course their true incompatibility will reveal itself as prayer departs.

61. When I examine my heart, when I behold my false repentance, I can say to the Lord only, "My God, I have never made any beginning in prayer!"

62. We know that we must repent, yet irrationally we fail to do it. This is as St. Paul has said of himself: *What I am doing, I do not understand. For what I will to do, that I do not practice; but what I hate, that I do.*[31] Let us, then, make our own the words of

---

30 Cf. Genesis 11:1–9.
31 Romans 7:15.

the father of the demon-possessed child in the Gospel, who cried to the Saviour: *Lord, I believe; help my unbelief!*[32]

63. It is never too late to make a beginning in repentance, and so it is never too late to begin to pray. A thousand times we may have tried and failed, yet at every moment the saving Lord calls us toward His Father. Only let us remember that we *know neither the day nor the hour in which the Son of Man is coming,*[33] when we shall be called from this life to the soul's fearful judgment; so let the moment of our true repentance be now, today, at this moment and no other!

THE GARDEN OF THE HEART

64. Have you ever planted a garden? Then you are aware how much care goes into every act: the preparing of the soil, the sowing of the seed, the watering of the seedling, the pruning of the mature plant. So it must be with prayer. True prayer is not the accident of happenstance, but the ripe fruit of the well-tended garden of the heart.

65. What good is it to spread seed or pour water over untilled soil? The good farmer knows that dry and packed earth, if not broken up and tilled, will resist both seed and water. So too with our hearts: if we spread the seed and pour out the water of many prayers, but have not broken up the hard ground of our resistant hearts, such prayer will remain only on the surface, on our lips. It will not take hold, and will easily be cast away by the winds of temptation. But if we are attentive to the heart, using the ascetical arsenal as tools to break up the hard ground of our pride and to furrow the soil of our wills, then may prayer take root deep within, becoming the flower of a heart in which lives and thrives the Spirit of the living God.

---

[32] Mark 9:24.
[33] Matthew 25:13.

66. The Fathers teach us that the soil of prayer is watered by tears; yet on account of our sins, we often lack the blessing of these spiritual tears by which the saints have watered the earth. God will bless our struggle still, yet let us remember: a single tear, shed in the true repentance that comes from the Spirit, brings more nourishment to the parched earth of the heart than a thousand streams of words and thoughts.

67. Just as a farmer at times must bring in water from an external source, when his own well has run dry, so too we must have recourse to the repentance and humble piety of our Fathers when our own is weak. Their lives are a spring that can replenish the dry well of the heart, and which can provide the nourishment to refresh what is weak in us.

68. A farmer cannot create his own seed: seed always comes from the mature plant that produces it—it is always inherited, always received. This, too, should serve as a reminder for our life of prayer. The grace we seek cannot but be received, handed to us from the mature experience and living mystery of the Church.

69. As we are reminded in the Scriptures, we do not receive only the seed, but also the soil, the rain, the very earth, and the light of the sun from God.[34] The farmer seeing a full harvest, or the gardener a beautiful array in full bloom, can glory only in the joy that comes from being a participant in the Lord's work—of having a part in His creativity and budding of new life. So, too, with the garden of the heart: the Lord provides the soil, which is our very creatureliness, fashioned after His image and likeness. He provides the seed, which is the grace of true prayer in the Spirit. He offers the rain and the sun, which are the gifts of repentance and transfiguration. And then He hands us the hoe and says, "Till," calling us to ascesis and a life of spiritual action.

70. When the garden of the heart is tilled, when it is tended, it produces a hundredfold. A small seed produces not just a fine

---

34 Cf. Hebrews 6:7.

fruit or a beautiful flower, but a new life, joined to the life of the eternal God. It blossoms into Paradise. It refashions Eden in the heart, and man is called back to his Maker.

THE DIVINE MYSTERIES: THE NOURISHMENT OF PRAYER

71. Returning in this way to his Maker and Fashioner, man finds himself anew in the temple of true prayer. A man cannot pray apart from the presence of God, even as a son cannot receive the embrace of his father if he does not run to his father's house.[35] So must we run to our Father's dwelling-place, the Church, and receive our precious Christ fully, wholly, in Body and Blood. In this way we embrace the presence of God—or rather, God embraces us—and prayer has a foundation on which to grow.

72. True prayer is this banquet of the heart in Christ. Its plate is the holy diskos, its cup the divine chalice. Its table is the altar of bloodless sacrifice, and its banqueting hall the sanctuary of the living Lord.

73. The divine Mystery of our true thanksgiving is both the icon and the food of prayer. As the Lamb upon the altar is broken yet never divided,[36] the heart at prayer is broken by ascesis, yet never divided against itself. True prayer crushes the heart, yet does not break it. It crucifies the will, but offers this sacrifice in order that the will may be raised. And so we hear it proclaimed: "Let your hearts be on high," and we reply: "We lift them up unto the Lord."[37] Exultantly debased, and debasingly exalted, we receive our Saviour in body and in spirit.

74. In this manner, the divine services nourish us in commu-

---

35 Cf. Luke 15:18–20.

36 Cf. the priest's prayer at the fraction of the Lamb in the Divine Liturgy: "Broken and distributed is the Lamb of God, Who being broken is not divided, being eaten is not consumed, but sanctifies those who partake thereof."

37 From the Anaphora of the Divine Liturgy of St. John Chrysostom.

nion with Life and train the heart, mind, and body in genuine prayer. Run to the temple, if you wish to convert and make stalwart the heart!

75. Each of the Church's Mysteries nourishes and feeds the life of prayer, and thus we must have recourse to all as best suits the needs of soul and body. Among these we must particularly remember regular Confession, by which the heart is lightened of the burdens that weigh it down with worldly cares. Without the practice of such Confession of thoughts and sins, we fetter to the earth that which might otherwise ascend to the heights of heaven.

76. Prayer is the sacrament of the heart. Our bodies are washed in Baptism, anointed by chrism and oil; our souls, having been cleansed and sealed by the Spirit through Baptism and Chrismation, are liberated through Confession. The Eucharist joins us, body and soul, to the incarnate Lord. And prayer transforms the receptive heart into the vessel and throne of God.

77. The training ground of prayer is the cell, for the cell is the icon of the heart. But the cell is made more spacious than all the cosmos because, through participation in the sacred Mysteries, the heart that struggles within it is united to the infinite and uncontainable God. It is only in the fully sacramental life that the cell is a fruitful plot; but by this life, it can bear more fruit than any other.[38]

MAKING A FRUITFUL BEGINNING

78. For all that we hear of the heights of prayer, we must not become arrogant or deluded. Let us not be exalted by words that are too lofty, which serve only to give the lie to our true condition, fallen and debased as we have in our transgression made it.

---

[38] And this is true not only of the monastic's cell, but of the cell of our Christian struggle wherever it may be quietly, attentively kept—whether in the home or in the monastery.

Rather, receiving from the Church and her saints the icon of the heights prayer can attain, let us return to our own hearts, taking our first steps in prayer, and ask God to give us a productive, simple beginning.

79. Great advances and many steps made in the growth of prayer are easily defeated by a single second of pride. Be on guard, lest this small enemy creep in through the gates and defeat you.

80. Only a heart that is broken can be mended. Pray to the Lord that He will help you crucify your heart. Then, at times of prayer, lay it quietly in the tomb of your mind, stilled of all thoughts, and wait upon the Lord of its resurrection.

81. Do not fritter about in times of prayer, worrying whether your clothes are just so, the lights just right, the candles properly arranged, your books all in order. When it is time to pray, pray.

82. Who can know the mystery of God? How different are God's ways than man's! God makes Himself present to the sinful heart, and purifies it by His radiant fire. He cleanses what cannot be cleansed, heals what cannot be healed; He restores to life what is already dead. He makes the impossible ascent of prayer possible to the feeblest of human hearts. Glory be to our man-befriending Lord!

83. Breathe in the Lord: let His presence be the beginning and end of every breath. Fill your heart, as your lungs, with His life, which is so near to hand. Consider every breath wasted which is not the new work of the Spirit, breathing true life into the dust of your nostrils and making of you a living being.[39]

84. If too many words (including those of this little text) distract or confuse your heart, remember that the whole Paradise of prayer is contained in the cry of the tax-collector: *God, be merciful to me, a sinner!*[40] By such a prayer of divine simplicity, many have attained the Kingdom of God.

---

39 Cf. Genesis 2:7.
40 Luke 18:13.

A Concluding Triad on Faith, Hope, and Love

And now abide faith, hope and love, these three;
but the greatest of these is love.[41]

FAITH

85. Let us hear the words of the great Apostle, and see how they speak to us of prayer. Faith, for its part, stands at the beginning of prayer. It is *the substance of things hoped for, the evidence of things not seen;*[42] and when our sight is not yet such as to see God face-to-face, faith draws our prayer close to the unseen God and accustoms us to dwell in His presence.

86. By faith our ancestors were led out of the wilderness into *the land of promise.*[43] By faith they were led to the sacred cities. By faith they were led from the cities to the deserts, and by faith from the desert to the Kingdom of God. So wherever we may be in our prayer—the wilderness of confusion, the city of stability, or the desert of true freedom—faith will lead us further toward salvation.

87. Faith is the fatherland of prayer. It is its home, its country, and its territory of fertile growth.

88. Faith calls down upon us the grace of God, and so waters the soil of prayer.

89. Where faith sows a seed, a great plant will grow. Even if the seed is small, or the smallest of them all,[44] great shoots may arise. And the plant that grows from the seed of faithful prayer is the very Tree of Life, the source of hope and eternal rejoicing. Let us seek out, then, the speck of faith that remains through our

---

[41] I Corinthians 13:13.
[42] Hebrews 11:1.
[43] Cf. Hebrews 11:8–9, 23–29.
[44] Cf. Matthew 13:31–32—the parable of the mustard seed.

sin and our blindness. The Lord will make of it a seed capable of planting Eden in the heart.

HOPE

90. Together with faith abides hope, its partner and friend, which guides it from the present to the future. Hope takes the faithful heart and moves it ever towards the Coming One and the Kingdom which is to come. Hope picks up faith, gives it legs, and pushes it toward its object and aim.

91. Our prayer, given its body by faith, thus receives its motion from hope. Hope moves our prayer beyond the tongue, beyond the mind, into the heart—for we know that in the heart it will journey further still: into the Kingdom which has no end.

92. Hope lives in the Kingdom. It lives at the end, even as it stands in the present—just as Christ once said to the repentant thief, *Today thou shalt be with Me in Paradise.*[45] So prayer, nourished by hope, lives today in the *parousia* of the tender Lord.

93. True hope is not expectation, but knowledge and surety. In this way, genuine hope is the stability of prayer.

94. Prayer that is rooted in sure hope is no longer tossed to and fro by desires, by passions, or by worldly concerns. It is grafted into the Lord, ever moving toward and residing in Him; and so it has the stability to give rise to the highest of virtues.

LOVE

95. Higher than that which resides solely in faith and hope is that prayer which exists also in the embrace of love, to which these give rise; for love knits the heart to God and makes of prayer a true communion of life in Life.

96. Love is the truest language of prayer, for love is the language that needs no language, no words, but only the gentle rest and uninterrupted communion of the purified heart.

---

45 Luke 23:43.

97. Bound to love, upheld by love, prayer becomes unceasing: it never ends and never fails.[46]

98. Without love, my prayer—whether made with words or without—sounds only as a *clanging symbol.*[47] Without love, my prayer is a dry well. Without love, my prayer stands alone, stands only with itself. But with love, my heart finds what is good, what is patient, what is kind:[48] it finds God Who is love,[49] borne within—and entertains this communion in its deepest chambers.

99. If faith, even the faith of a mustard seed, can move the mountains,[50] how much more can the heart infused with divine love transform the cosmos!

GLORY TO GOD, THE HOLY TRINITY

100. Let us, then, who seek to make a beginning in prayer, rush to God with hearts rich in the fervor of love, even if this love be yet untrained and imperfect. The Lord Himself will kindle love's flame in our heart, and we shall find ourselves wholly His. He will offer us true prayer, by which and in which we will receive His love and love Him all the more. Glory to this God of love! Glory to this pre-eternal King, to Whom we pray and Who prays in us: Father, Son and Holy Spirit, now and ever, and to the ages of ages.

AMEN!

✛

---

46 Cf. I Corinthians 13:8.
47 Cf. I Corinthians 13:1.
48 Cf. I Corinthians 13:4–7.
49 Cf. I John 4:8, 16.
50 Cf. Matthew 17:20.

A Second Century on Prayer:
On the Preparation of the Mind and Heart

BECOMING GUARDIANS OF THE HEART AND MIND

1. Prayer is a divine gift and blessed grace. The heart which God has fashioned from the dust, into which He has breathed His own breath, is called beyond the confines of mere materiality. The mystery of the separation between Creator and creature is overcome, as the Maker and Fashioner of the human heart calls it to Himself.

2. When the heart responds to this call and is drawn up into God, it finds its true home, peace, and joy. This is as St. Seraphim of Sarov reminded his hearers: "When the mind and heart are united in prayer and the soul's thoughts are not dispersed, the heart is warmed by spiritual warmth in which the light of Christ shines, making the whole inner man peaceful and joyous. We should thank the Lord for everything and give ourselves up to His will; we should likewise offer Him all our thoughts, words, and actions, and strive to make everything serve only His good pleasure."[1]

3. To unite the mind and heart in prayer as the Saint instructs, a discipline of interior quietude is required—for normally our mind and our heart reside distantly from one another, unwittingly content in their disassociation. This condition we

---

[1] St. Seraphim of Sarov, "Spiritual Instructions to Laymen and Monks," in *Little Russian Philokalia,* vol. 1: *St. Seraphim of Sarov,* trans. Fr. Seraphim Rose (Platina, Calif.: St. Herman of Alaska Brotherhood, 1978; 5th edition, 2008).

are called to address, as the Persian Sage says: "From the moment you start praying, raise your heart upward and turn your eyes downward. Bring your focus to your innermost self, and there pray in secret to your heavenly Father."[2]

4. Our prayer, if it is to be effective and to grow from beginnings to maturity, must move from the "rooftop" of the lips to the "secret chambers" of our innermost heart.[3] Of this the Sage again makes us aware: "Our Lord instructed us to pray in secret—this means, in our heart—and also to 'shut the door.'[4] What is this door he says we must shut, if not the mouth? For we are the temple in which Christ dwells, for so the Apostle said, *Ye are the temple of God*.[5] The Lord enters into your inner self, into this house, to cleanse it from everything that is unclean; but only when the door, that is your mouth, is closed shut."[6]

5. Thus we are taught that there is a need to stand guard, if we are to make progress in prayer: to guard the lips, the mind, and the heart. In this, however, we often fail—and hence our prayer does not grow. How can we expect our heart fruitfully to be God's temple, if we allow into it with reckless abandon those thoughts and desires and other invaders who would occupy it instead?

6. There is a need, rather, to become good watchers of the heart, as well as the mind; to discern that which is good and fosters our prayer from that which rends it from us. This is the spiritual labor of disciplined prayer, and is the preparation by which we draw near to God.

7. So let us rise up to the task and learn to stand guard against those inward opponents to prayer: our wayward thoughts and

---

[2] Venerable Aphrahat the Persian (commemorated January 29), *Demonstration on Prayer*, 4.13.

[3] Cf. Matthew 6:1–6.

[4] Cf. Matthew 6:6.

[5] I Corinthians 3:16.

[6] Venerable Aphrahat the Persian, *Demonstration on Prayer*, 4.10.

distractions of the mind and heart. Let us apply ourselves to the discipline required to receive Him Who desires to make His abode within us, Who longs to be our only love and good.

Peace, solace, and pressure

ON THE QUIETING OF THE THOUGHTS IN PRAYER

8. To foster the heart in prayer and seek this guardianship of the interior life, one must first strive to calm the thoughts. The constant movement of the mind prevents it from entering into the heart, which is the only place where it may find true peace and solace. When, instead, the mind remains separate, fuelled only by its thoughts as if by a worldly food, it never finds its rest in God.

9. Such thoughts are among our greatest distractions in prayer. Often when we stand or sit to pray, it is not a coldness of heart that defeats us, nor a lack of will, nor a feebleness of character. It is, rather, the constant flood of thoughts that conquers the mind, which we realize we have little ability to control.

10. To overcome this obstacle to prayer, we must develop in ourselves a custom of guarding the heart through calming the thoughts. This calming of the thoughts comes only after a long time spent in discerning the good from the bad in the power of the mind. We cannot aim for the highest good, of quieting all thought and entering into the wordless silence of thought-less prayer, without first learning to approach silence by a gradually increasing quietude.

11. Quietude, then, is a necessary ingredient for the development of prayer, not merely at the times dedicated to this divine act, but as an overriding characteristic of our Life in Christ. If we are constantly talkative and noisy in our worldly affairs, then this is the spirit we will bring to our prayer—and the constant stream of words by which we are distracted in our day-to-day conversations will become a constant stream of thoughts by which we are distracted in our attempt to sit quietly in the presence of God.

12. The calming of the thoughts has a practical beginning, then, in the seeking out of a quieter way of life. Though we may live in the midst of the world with all its noise and distractions, it is not primarily our surroundings that dictate whether or not we live in quietude, but our inner approach and behavior. If we respond to the noise of the world with a quiet mouth and gentle spirit, quiet stillness is created in our heart.

13. Without such quietude, which the Fathers call *hesychia,* we do not even realize how dominated we are by our thoughts. With it, we at last are given eyes to see how they flood through us and out of us with such abandon. Such quietude is not the answer to the dominance of our wayward thoughts, but it is the context in which we may overcome them. Once we become still, we can see the turmoil our uncontrolled thoughts present to our prayer.

14. Before we obtain some small degree of quietude, we stand to pray and naïvely believe we are wholly focused on the Lord our Saviour; but after we have tasted of this precious stillness, we stand before God and realize that our attention is pulled in countless directions, often going—unwittingly—to places dark and far from divine grace. So a calmed and quiet heart enables us to see our struggle as it really is, and so make a beginning in its true improvement.

PRACTICAL STEPS TO THE QUIETING
OF THE MIND AND HEART

15. How do we find this quieter way of life? Begin by contributing quietude to a world of noise and disarray. Savor silence when the world wills you to speak. This is as one of the Fathers has said: "If you wish to make a spiritual pilgrimage, begin by closing your mouth."[7]

---

7 From the *Sayings of the Egyptian Fathers,* 72 (PL 74.391); in *The Book of Mystical Chapters,* ed. John Anthony McGuckin (Boston: Shambhala, 2003), Praktikos 67, p. 47.

16. Learn to love opportunities not to speak, not to contribute, not to influence. Rather than crave conversations in which your voice can be heard, crave instead those opportunities in which your silence may respond to voice, in which you may sacrifice your willful desire for self-involvement on the altar of quiet humility before God and man.

17. When there is no need to speak, do not speak!

18. Seek to console your brother in two words, rather than ten (unless he requires more; and then, do what is required for the salvation of your brother). Seek to be consoled by one word, rather than two. Strive to curb your need for wordiness—either in offering or receipt—and encourage the tongue, your own as well as your brother's, to be at rest unless God calls it to action.

19. Do not fill your mind with worldly noise without reason. Radios or televisions operating "in the background" prevent quietude by filling even empty moments with the distracting flow of sounds and voices. How shall we find quiet in our times of prayer, if we have so conditioned ourselves against it in every other moment?

20. Take full advantage of the means given by the Church to enable focused quiet in the heart. Long vigil is not simply devotional: it is a practical measure to curb the uncontrolled diversions of the world with the controlled and intentional words of divine life. Similarly, the rule given to us by our spiritual father is not an obedience alone: it is also a tool to train the mind on that which is singular and good, rather than allow it to wander amidst its own noise and confusion. Take up these tools, by which stillness and quietude are presented for our possession!

21. Remember at all times how powerful was our Lord's silence in His earthly life. With silence He rebuked those who meant to condemn the woman caught in adultery.[8] With silence

---

[8] Cf. John 8:2–11.

how much distress in my life could have been avoided through silence.

THE BEGINNINGS OF A LIFE OF PRAYER

He replied to Pilate's demands for truth.[9] *As a lamb before its shearer is silent, so He opened not His mouth.*[10] Thus He Who was silent conquered sin and death and all the forces of evil. Strive with all your power to obtain a taste of this powerful quietude that conquers every stirring of the evil one!

Developing an Awareness of the Power of Thoughts

22. The quiet we seek to engender in our lives will lead, by God's good mercy, to an awareness of the power of our thoughts, and the need to calm them if we are to grow in prayer and communion in the Holy Trinity. The helpmeet of quietude thus brings us to a second step in the curbing of the thoughts: an awareness of their force and power.

23. This awareness first comes in the form of a simple, experiential knowledge that there is a force to the thoughts which has not yet come under the control of the heart. A quiet heart shows up the noise and mayhem of the thoughts. When first we come to see this, we are too weak to combat the thoughts' strange power and defeat it. At this stage, however, it is enough that we step out of the darkness of ignorance into the light of awareness, and acknowledge this power which previously had affected us unawares.

24. The longer we dwell in examining the movements of the mind, the more we see that the activity of the thoughts is in fact what gives them their force. The thoughts reign because they are always active and know no rest.

25. When, however, we begin to become aware of the thoughts' power and their activity, we must not grow despondent. A prerequisite for spiritual healing is a right perception of

---

9 Cf. John 18:38; Matthew 27:14; Mark 15:5.
10 Isaiah 53:7. Cf. Acts 8:32.

our illness, and inasmuch as we are held captive by uncontrolled thoughts, we are spiritually ill.

26. Do not be surprised when, as this awareness develops in you, you find many temptations to interior turmoil, upset, and distraction. We have been blind to our ailment so long that we have learned to ignore it; but once it is revealed to us, it can no longer be ignored and we fear we may be overcome by its magnitude. But *be not afraid, only believe,* says the Lord.[11] This is a natural and expected response to the new attentiveness of the heart; trust that the Lord of the heart will protect you from this temptation that accompanies spiritual growth.

27. Rather than despair at the magnitude of our thoughts' power, as yet still uncontrolled and dominating in our interior life, cry out instead with the sinner, *Mine iniquities are gone over my head; as a heavy burden they are too much for me!*[12] and believe that the Lord will redeem you from this captivity. You have always been thus bound: rejoice inasmuch as now you see the contours of your mind's captivity, and can respond to the true condition of your life!

28. The thoughts have power, and in their tumultuous activity this power is great; but the Lord has more power still. He Who calmed the seas with a word[13] will calm this tumult also. As your eyes are newly opened to the depth of your struggle, cling with new fervor to the Lord of your salvation! He desires your prayer, your abode in Him—and He will release you from every chain that binds you.

EXAMINING THE THOUGHTS OBJECTIVELY

29. The ultimate aim in developing an awareness of the thoughts' activity and power is to be able to calm and quiet them,

---

[11] Mark 5:36.
[12] Psalm 37:5.
[13] Cf. Mark 4:35–41.

so that true prayer can blossom. To calm the thoughts, then, the next step in this spiritual discipline is for a man to examine his mind as if it were a book on which are written the constant flow of these words and images pouring out from his intellect. Rather than be held captive by these thoughts as they issue forth from the mind, set them out and examine them, each in its own measure.

30. Without scrutiny, there is no way to defeat the uncontrolled flow of thoughts into the heart.

31. In this examination of the thoughts, we must strive for objectivity in our attentive observation. The thoughts that come into our mind dominate our spiritual lives because we are subject to them and know them only subjectively. But when we are able to examine our thoughts objectively, as if from the outside, we are given the grace to begin to discern the good from the bad, the healthy from the unhealthy.

32. Our attentive gaze on the activity of the mind must take the form of a dispassionate judge reviewing the facts of cases set before him. As one removed from events, he is able to discern their value. So it must be with our examination of our thoughts: we must seek to identify the good and the evil dispassionately, so that we may welcome the former and dismiss the latter without clinging to either.

33. Look carefully at each thought as it enters your mind. Whence does it come? What is its origin and source? To what does it lead—to God or to perdition? Accept as friends those thoughts that come as well-invited guests and draw you toward the Lord of the heart; but reject as impostors and uninvited wedding guests those whose origins are in the passions and who seek to pull your heart from God and enslave it to the world.[14]

34. When your attentive gaze deems a thought good and holy, a welcome guest at the banquet of your heart, bid it past the guard-post of your discriminating intellect. But there is a dif-

---

[14] Cf. Matthew 22:1–14.

ference between allowing a good thought to settle in the heart, and latching onto it as an object of your attention and mental activity. Accept what comes from God as His gift, and remain vigilant. Do not cling even to the good, past what is fitting. The weak mind can make idols even out of the good.

35. Once we have gained—through the familiarity of long practice and the guidance of blessed instruction and direction—the ability to repel and dismiss those thoughts which would trouble the heart, we instead water its depths only with those thoughts that come from God. These are thoughts which have their origins in the divine and aim at the virtues, and each blesses the heart with a new closeness to its Maker, in which mental activity is no longer our chief good. In this manner, holy thoughts breed the stillness we seek in prayer.

On Dismissing Wayward Thoughts

36. We have already said that we must resist the temptation to cling too strongly to the good when such thoughts enter into our mind at prayer, for such possession directs us away from God Himself. Our aim is not to cling to good thoughts, but to God alone.

37. Similarly, when resisting those thoughts which are unwelcome, do not allow this act to become itself a new mental occupation, keeping you from dwelling on the love of the Lord. A battle against distraction that keeps us from resting in God's presence and abiding in Him, is itself a spiritual distraction.

38. You should not seek to combat your evil thoughts, in the sense of waging a direct, focused warfare against them: they will often get the best of you—for we stand together as weak men, little able to wage battle directly against the powers that would destroy us. Instead, strive not to combat but to dismiss those thoughts which come into the mind seeking to trouble the heart. Such is more consonant with the instruction of our Fathers.

39. To dismiss a wayward thought is to refuse it entry into the sacred space of our inner life, where it will wreak havoc on the stillness of the heart. Yet it is not to draw the powers of the heart out to resist it, which equally disrupts interior stillness. It is, rather, simply sending it on its way when it makes itself known; calmly refusing entry to one who has no place in the house, and thus not allowing it to disturb the peace that reigns within.

40. If we turn all our attention towards the struggle against unwelcome thoughts, we feed them by our focus and energize them with the power of our own spirit. Thus small distractions, fed by our attention and focus, become great, and the powers that might have left us unharmed become foes that ensnare us all the more.

41. Therefore do not feed the thoughts by undue focus and attention. Once a thought is identified as good, give thanks to God and move on, letting the heart above all cherish its rest in the Lord. Once a thought is identified as bad, dismiss it as unwelcome, give thanks to God for this gifted preservation, and renew your attentive gaze over the mind. In this way, you cut away the root and source of spiritual power from those thoughts that would overwhelm you, and they quickly wither and cease to pose spiritual danger. A thought that is not fed by attention speedily dies.

42. By practicing such vigilance in the observation of thoughts and the dismissal of those that would captivate us, we begin by God's grace to curb the formerly uncontrolled activity of the mind. The stream of thoughts that previously flowed unrestrained into the heart, allowing every wayward distraction to find a home there and grow, is now divided, so that only those thoughts of good, of God Himself, find entry and all the rest are diverted away. And so we will find that those thoughts which find no home in the heart soon cease to present themselves to it, and the mind is gradually stilled of this unwanted activity, more

purely taking comfort and refuge in the continual remembrance of its Maker and Fashioner.

On Dismissing Specific Types of Thoughts

43. Practical steps are of aid in dismissing specific categories of thoughts that often plague the heart. When thoughts of lust are identified, recognize these as perversions of the good desire God has fashioned in your heart, intended for the unbending longing for union with Him. Seeing the lustful thought in this manner, rather than as an inexplicable yet powerful reality of its own, allows it to be dismissed not as a great lion stalking at the door, but simply as a wrong use of the gifts God has given us. We will send it away, welcoming it back only when it has become true desire for the God of life.

44. When thoughts of despondency or despair, sometimes called depression, are identified, once more observe them not as strange and sourceless spiritual evils, but as instances of the mind's power being unduly turned in on itself, seeing only its limitation and finitude, and not the eternal and great majesty of God. Send such thoughts on their way with the gentle insistence that, though you may not see Him now, you know God is near at hand, *with you always, even to the end of the age,*[15] and do not allow their poison to enter your heart.

45. When thoughts come upon you that inspire you toward loneliness and self-pity, dismiss them with the calm reminder that God is "everywhere present," that He has fashioned you from the dust and has known you from your mother's womb,[16] that He is always with you and closer to you than your nearest kin or dearest friend. Send such thoughts on their way as unwelcome in their lies; for your heart knows better than to trust in their foolishness.

---

[15] Matthew 28:20.
[16] Cf. Genesis 2:7; Jeremiah 1:5.

46. If the thoughts that come upon you are of jealousy concerning those benefits and gifts that you have observed in others (and the thoughts that pour forth uncontrolled from the mind are often of this type), dismiss them with the assurance that the Lord apportions to each and to all as is meet for their salvation, in the good timing and order of His divine mercy. The world had long cried out for the coming of its Saviour, but the Lord was born of the Theotokos *when the time had fully come.*[17] So send thoughts of jealousy on their way with the soft reply of their irrationality. No benefit or grace could more be desired for you than that which the Lord gives and shall give, according to His love for you!

47. If the thoughts that come upon you are of arrogance or pride, which emulate the Pharisee in saying, *I thank Thee, O God, that I am not like other men,*[18] or otherwise call you toward self-exaltation and reliance, call to heart the words of St. Silouan: "Where there is pride there cannot be grace, and if we lose grace we also lose both love of God and assurance in prayer. The soul is then tormented by evil thoughts and does not understand that she must humble herself and love her enemies, for there is no other way to please God."[19] Instead, remember your lowliness before the majesty of God, and cry out in humility with the words of the same Saint: "What shall I render unto Thee, O Lord, for that Thou hast poured such great mercy on my soul? Grant, I beg Thee, that I may see my iniquities, and ever weep before Thee, for Thou art filled with love for humble souls, and dost give them the grace of the Holy Spirit."[20]

---

[17] Galatians 4:4.

[18] Luke 18:11.

[19] St. Silouan of Mt. Athos, as found in Archimandrite Sophrony, *St. Silouan the Athonite,* trans. Rosemary Edmonds (Essex, England: Stavropegic Monastery of St. John the Baptist, 1991; reprint Crestwood, N.Y.: St. Vladimir's Seminary Press), p. 378.

[20] Ibid., p. 381.

48. If the thoughts that come upon you are of greed, of the desire for possessions or comforts or other such things—even if these things be holy and presented under the guise of aids to your spiritual life—remember that those who had nothing have entered the Kingdom, that the meek have inherited the earth,[21] and that the rich have become paupers and been sent empty away.[22]

49. In such manners do we dismiss the captivating power of these thoughts by stripping them of their force: a force primarily grounded in deception. A quiet heart examines the true nature of such temptations, and dismisses them without aggression as foreigners to the spiritual life and to the true communion of prayer. Thus they gain no entry into the heart, which rather than harboring these unwanted guests instead plays host to the King and Lord of all.

The Leaving Behind of Judgment

50. Amongst the most difficult and pernicious of all the thoughts that come upon us in times of prayer (as indeed at many other times) are those of judgment: judgment against our brethren for their wrongs, their faults, their shortcomings. Thoughts enter into our mind that remind us of failings we have witnessed or believe we have identified, and these furrow their way into our heart and occupy our attention with great force. For this reason, they must be dismissed at the first sign of their advent, before they gain any footing in our interior life. The moment they are allowed entrance to the heart, the spiritual battle for prayer is lost.

51. Judgment of a brother kills prayer. It destroys even the beginnings of prayer—that ardent desire and longing to abide

---

[21] Cf. Matthew 5:5.
[22] Cf. Luke 1:53.

in God and rest in Him—for in judging we create in ourselves not the opportunity for union with the Trinity, but division and separation from the Lord.

52. When the Lord commands us, *Judge not, lest ye be judged,*[23] let this be for us a guide and rule to prayer. Should the just Master judge our heart rightly, we would find ourselves cast into the outer darkness, where the union of true prayer is neither a hope nor a possibility. Yet in His love He overlooks our sin and offers divine forgiveness. So let us likewise dismiss judgment and with it all condemnation of our brethren, so that we may exercise divine love and grow closer to God.

53. When your heart seeks to judge because of these thoughts that pour into it, remember the manner in which you have been judged. You deserve from God only perdition and death; yet the judgment He has shown you is the Cross—His ultimate act of love and self-offering. Only such self-sacrificial judgment has a place in the heart of God. Would you harbor any other in your own heart, and still claim to grow in prayer that is union with Him?

54. It is impossible to love God if we do not love our neighbor, and it is impossible to love our neighbor if judgment is our secret greeting and the substance of our hidden relationship with him. Do not claim to pray, or even to be a Christian, if your heart fosters any judgment of your brother!

55. Instead, when thoughts and temptations of judgment arise in the mind, quiet them with the sign of the Cross and the remembrance of the One Who died upon it "for the life and salvation of the world."[24] Cast out this poison before it gains any entry, and your prayer can be saved.

---

[23] Matthew 7:1.

[24] Cf. the prayer of the priest at the preparation of the Lamb during the Proskomedia: "Sacrificed is the Lamb of God, Who taketh away the sin of the world, for the life of the world and for its salvation."

56. Remember that in refusing to judge a brother, we foster in ourselves forgiveness, which draws us closer to our Redeemer. Take solace in the words attributed to St. Theophan the Recluse: "Nothing is so powerful in the sight of the Lord as the forgiving of offenses, because it is the imitation of one of the actions closest to us of God's mercifulness." By dismissing judgment and fostering forgiveness, the heart strives for God's love. So we also hear: "The forgiving of offenses is a most attractive virtue, often bringing into the heart a reward for itself."

THE CONTINUAL REMEMBRANCE OF THE NAME OF JESUS

57. When, by quiet attentiveness, we have begun to dismiss those thoughts which come upon us unaware and have begun to restrain the constant activity of the mind, we must then take the newly cleared chamber of the heart and fill it with that for which it most ardently longs: the presence and remembrance of the Name of Jesus Christ. This is the Name which is *above every name,* at which *every knee shall bow,*[25] and the heart itself shall embrace it as dearest friend and closest companion. With it the heart will cry out to the Lord of all, and welcome Him into His temple.

58. We may at times, indeed many times, have called upon the Name of the Lord in our prayer and ascesis; but until the thoughts had been restrained in prayer and the heart made ready, this Name with all its divine power was thrust into the general disarray of our inner life. We were, in this way, like the man who took the pearl of great price and buried it in the dirt, amongst so many other stones and rocks. But when the heart is made still and prepared, then the receipt of this Name, as its singular focus and good, takes up the substance of the heart and transfigures it with divine glory.

---

[25] Cf. Philippians 2:9, 10.

59. The Fathers tell us to attach the Name, in the form of the Jesus Prayer, to our very breath.[26] Do not take this counsel as suggesting to you some system or technique; rather, receive it instead as the basic instruction that the Name of Jesus should be as familiar to us as our own breath. You do not consciously "remember" to breathe: it is a function of your person, without which your body cannot survive. So also should it be with our calling upon the Lord's holy Name, without which the soul does not know the true Life of its Maker. By attaching the one to the other, we unite in us what is important to body as well as soul.

60. This closeness of the Name to the breath can only come about through long discipline, by which the constant repetition of the prayer creates of it a habit of the heart. For this reason, cling to the rule by which your prayer is ordered and made regular. Run to your rule each day as the arena in which the Name of the Lord is worked into your soul.

61. The Name of the Lord Jesus Christ has immense power. Do not forget that in each utterance of it, you are given grace to speak the unutterable glory of God, to proclaim the incarnation, to announce redemption and salvation to your heart and to all the world. The Name of the Lord is transfiguring, for in a word it announces creation, sin, redemption, and all eternity; and it is a confession of the One Who has made prayer possible.

62. But the Name of the Saviour is also precious and tender. Its majesty is incomparable, but its intimacy indescribable. The true Name of Him Who fashioned all things rests upon the lips, within the heart. While in all Israel none but the Great High Priest could speak the Name for reason of its splendor and holiness, we who are the New Israel are not only permitted but commanded to call tenderly upon the Lord by name. Look, how near to hand the Lord has come!

---

[26] The Jesus Prayer in its customary form: "Lord Jesus Christ, Son of God, have mercy on me, a sinner."

63. When our heart truly dwells in the Name of the Lord, we begin to foster in ourselves the very intimacy by which prayer is taken from its beginnings to the deeper communion for which we long. The Lord has come near to us, and so we draw near to Him, responding to love with love and welcoming the transfiguring closeness of the Saviour.

On Intercessions for Others and the Silence of Prayer

64. As by God's grace our prayer makes its beginning and starts to grow, the Lord reveals to the heart how it may intercede for the world in the new context of its quiet rest in Him. For as we grow closer to Christ, so we grow closer to all His creation and particularly His children, to Whom we are newly united as sons and daughters of the risen Lord.

65. As prayer becomes purer and simpler, resting more and more completely in God and separating itself from all worldly cares, it does not abandon the world. Rather, the heart which wholly adores its Maker yearns, with Him and in Him, for the salvation of all mankind—and even for the whole of creation itself. It yearns to draw all that is fallen and broken toward completion and sanctification in Christ.

66. When our prayer begins, we remember those for whom we intercede through words and thoughts. This is a gift and grace, which echoes our liturgical prayer in the Church. Embrace this responsibility with humility and spiritual joy, and do not let your prayer grow cold through lack of love.

67. Then, as discipline yields a growth in prayer, we may find—should God will it—that our intercession and commemoration of those for whom we pray may itself come in quieter form: by calling them to mind in the depths of the heart, as the heart rests quietly in the embrace of the Holy Trinity. No words need forge our intercession. It is enough (nay, it is far

greater) that we draw them into that communion in God that is nurtured deep within.

68. Prayer is a mystery: behold its mysterious dimensions! In the human heart, God makes a welcome dwelling; and in this same heart, we may make a deposit of the living memory of all those who seek our prayer, though we be unworthy of that charge. In this heart, God and neighbor meet; brethren and kin are brought together; friend and stranger are united. Seek to draw all the world into your heart, for the heart that is made ready to receive God Himself has room in its chambers for the whole of His creation.

69. The prayer of interior silence, then, is the true prayer of love. *Love thy neighbor,*[27] *honor thy father and thy mother,*[28] *serve ye one another:*[29] all these commandments are fulfilled in the heart that truly prays. He who has become a pastor within the heart is true neighbor and friend and brother, and good servant to his fellow members in the Body of Christ.

70. Let us then betake ourselves to prayer, not merely for our own sake, but for that of our brethren. Let us attain the peace within by which a thousand around us may find salvation.[30] Let us rise to the work of interior stillness, that a troubled world may find rest, and we, too, attain to the Kingdom of God!

On Prayer without Thoughts

71. We have spoken about the thoughts, and the need to discern the good from the bad so that the heart may be kept

---

[27] Matthew 22:39. Cf. Leviticus 19:18.

[28] Exodus 20:12; Deuteronomy 5:16; Matthew 15:4; Mark 7:10, 19; Luke 18:20.

[29] Galatians 5:13.

[30] Cf. perhaps the most well-known of all St. Seraphim of Sarov's sayings: "Acquire the Spirit of peace within you, and a thousand around you will be saved."

pure and quieted for communion in the Holy Spirit, allowing into the chamber of the heart only that which is *true and
noble, just and pure and lovely, and of good report ... dwelling on
these things.*[31] Yet the Holy Fathers tell us that beyond even this
purified state of calm contemplation of the good is the highest
form of prayer: that which is without thought, going beyond all
word, form, and image entirely. This is the "wordless prayer" of
the purest heart.

72. We should maintain at all times an awareness of this highest form of prayer, in which the beginnings are brought to their
fullest maturity, so that we do not go astray in our discipline.
One must know the aim toward which he shoots. Yet, at the
same time, we must recognize that such thought-less, wordless
prayer is the full fruit of intense discipline and ascesis; it is the
foretaste of the Kingdom in this life. Woe to him who believes he
can attain this goal without the long struggles of obedience, self-
sacrifice, and preparation required of the Life in Christ!

73. Many, out of an unrestrained piety, fall into the trap of
seeking prayer without thoughts as a first aim. This is because
we know of the descriptions of such a good, but do not possess
the discernment to know our own degree of maturity and spiritual growth. When, however, such prayer is attempted before its
time, it leads immediately to delusion. It is impossible for a mind
to be without thoughts, without words or images, until it has
learned to control and restrain its activity. This can only come
about through the discipline of observation, dismissal of the bad,
and dwelling on the good.

74. Once this discipline becomes habit, then even the good
thoughts can be dismissed, as the heart learns to dwell in the
immediate presence of its Creator. But without the discipline to
establish this true communion, the heart will dwell only in its
self-deception.

---

[31] Cf. Philippians 4:8.

75. We must not believe ourselves more advanced than we are. Rather, we must always consider ourselves beginners, taking the first steps toward the Kingdom. The way toward thought-less prayer is that of obedience and discipline. Embrace these, do not deny them! When and if our hearts are ready, God will call us further.

76. It is part of the mystery of our growth in Christ that the right use of words can lead to wordless communion; that the disciplining of thoughts can lead to prayer without them. What a glorious mystery is the path of our salvation!

77. Only do not lose sight of our lofty aim! True communion in Christ is that for which our heart longs, and God desires nothing more than to grant such holy desires of the heart. So work while it is still day,[32] that the heart may find its solace and satisfaction in the love of God!

Do Not Fear: God Seeks Your Growth in Prayer

78. Do not be afraid of the struggles that will befall you in making a beginning in true prayer. Wide is the road by which our prayer may remain shallow and superficial, but narrow is the way that leads the human heart to the direct embrace of its Maker.[33] Yet this way has been trod before us by the Son Himself, by countless saints, by inspired victors of the spiritual battle. Take heart: it is a way meant to be followed.

79. Consider each temptation as an opportunity for purification, for strengthening your quiet resolve and spiritual fortitude. He who never falls in prayer is making no real attempt at growth.

80. Prayer opens our eyes to the reality of the world in which we live, replete with the fearful presence of sin and death,

---

[32] Cf. John 9:4.
[33] Cf. Matthew 7:13–14.

destruction and sorrow. <u>Eyes purified by prayer see new depths of the tragedy of our condition.</u> Yet hear the words of our Saviour: *Fear not, little flock, for it is your Father's good pleasure to give you the Kingdom.*[34] From all things Christ redeems us, for He has loved what He has seen truly—which now comes newly before your eyes.

81. Do not be afraid when prayer reveals to you the broken reality of the world, for Christ has overcome the world. It is His, and you are His!

82. There have been many whose fear has got the best of them, and who through fear have become stunted in their spiritual growth. The world preaches fear, and fear brings isolation and division; but God makes strong the heart of man, knowing that *an anxious heart weighs a man down*;[35] and He grants a love that *casts out fear.*[36] Therefore take refuge in God, Who will overcome every obstacle that keeps man far from Him.

83. Remember how the Apostle was given to partake in Christ's miracle, himself walking upon the water like his Lord and Master; yet when fear entered into his heart, he sank into the waves of the sea.[37] So it is with our prayer: when we trust in God and rest in Him, the grace of His divine power embraces us; but when we allow our hearts to be ruled by fear—whether worldly or spiritual—we cut ourselves away from this grace and begin to sink into the waters of worldly things.

84. Therefore do not be afraid! Let no temptation call you away from the life of prayer! Let no obstacle be for you a true menace! The Lord is victorious, *mighty in battle,*[38] and our very Defender: who can do us harm?

---

34 Luke 12:32.
35 Proverbs 12:25.
36 I John 4:18.
37 Cf. Matthew 14:28–33.
38 Cf. Psalm 23:8.

A Concluding Triad on the Guideposts of Prayer: The Cross, the Grave, and the Empty Tomb

The Cross

85. As we make a beginning in prayer and follow the guidance of the Church towards growth, let the central images of the Lord's Passion—the Cross, the grave, and the empty tomb—serve as guideposts along the way. For the Lord provides us here, too, with an example of the struggles that accompany our approach to divine life.

86. As at the Cross the Saviour felt the pains of the nails and the piercing of the spear, yet offered Himself willingly out of love for those who *do not know what they are doing,*[39] so our struggles in prayer will be accompanied by pains, even at times agonies. Yet that which calls us forward is love: the love God has shown us, and the love the heart desires to return to Him. So accept your little cross out of love, and do not become disheartened when pains and struggles accompany the life to which we are called.

87. The Cross was a willing condescension of the Lord, to take upon Himself humility, constraint, mockings, and true sacrifice. The approach to prayer will draw us into all of these, if it is to become that prayer which genuinely unites us to our crucified Saviour.

88. Especially when our prayer is at its beginnings, it must represent a crucifixion: a crucifixion of our will, our wayward desires, the false freedom of our uncontrolled thoughts, and our idle rest in those things which keep us from God. But so may it be to our glory, for in this way we grow closer to our Redeemer, Who was glorified upon the Tree.

89. Draw the Lord's Cross into your heart when you pray: do

---

[39] Luke 23:34.

not fear it. Though it is mighty and terrible, it is also the source of our life and our joy. Remember one truth above all else—a truth we have had cause to speak of before: "Through the Cross, joy has come into all the world";[40] and so it will come even into our lowly hearts.

THE GRAVE

90. As the Cross at Golgotha led our Lord to the tomb, to death and burial, so our prayer must follow Christ. Prayer will lead us to life, but the life we seek is one that comes through death. If you wish to pray, be prepared to die!

91. Our death is to be to this world in its sinful separation from God. We must die to our waywardness, to our self-will, to our false idols. We must die to a world that has taken death as its defining characteristic. Dying in this way, we open ourselves to life.

92. In following the example of the Lord, our death must also lead us to the grave and to burial. In His divine death, the Saviour was enclosed in the tomb and laid to rest; yet in that mysterious rest He entered hades and granted deliverance to those in bonds. So our death to the world in prayer must lead us to a similar rest, cut off from worldly concerns, so that our heart abides only in God. Then, in a great mystery, the heart thus "dead and buried" in Christ communes with all the living and all the dead—for *if we have died with Christ, we believe that we shall also live with Him,*[41] and we are united to the whole of His creation.

93. Seek after prayer that rests with God in the life-giving tomb. Do not long to be absent from the Lord's repose in the grave. Only seek that the death you foster to the world leads

---

[40] From the hymn at Sunday Matins, "Having beheld the Resurrection of Christ"; see above, *A Century on Prayer and Watchfulness,* §42, p. 83.

[41] Romans 6:8.

you to *His* rest, which is active and grace-bearing, not lifeless or dejected.

94. As prayer grows, the heart communes in the mystery of Christ's self-offering, itself becoming a tomb in which the Lord dwells. In the same way that the cave of the tomb, in the Church's holy icons, is indistinguishable from the cave of the Lord's saving birth, so the heart that has become a tomb to the world has also become a manger for the Lord of life.

The Empty Tomb

95. When, if by God's grace we are given to attain it, we grow in prayer as the Fathers direct, then the heart, which has died to the world and become a grave of saving repose, becomes a perfect icon of the empty tomb encountered by the holy myrrh-bearing women. It becomes a place which cannot restrain life, but which instead discloses the true power of Life to all the world.

96. The heart that has attained the heights of prayer is, like the empty tomb, a place which in its silence, its simplicity, its emptiness to worldly things shows forth the presence of the risen Lord. For the tomb of Christ was discovered empty, indeed; but its emptiness did not bear witness to a Lord Who was gone or absent. Rather, it proclaimed that He was risen, that He was and is eternally present, always with His creation. Thus the heart, transfigured by prayer, manifests the love and presence of God Who is Lord of the heart.

97. The empty tomb transformed the cosmos. So will the prayer of the heart transform the person, the cosmos, even all creation.

98. The empty tomb brought an end to death. So will true prayer bring an end to sorrow, to separation, to pain; for the resurrected Lord makes His abode in the heart, and the power witnessed in the empty tomb is manifest in the human creature.

99. Prayer is the communion of man in God. The mystery of

the Resurrection is fully disclosed in the heart of him who has attained prayer, and prayer enables the creature to declare from full experience: "Christ is risen! Truly, He is risen!"[42]

GLORY TO GOD, THE HOLY TRINITY

100. Let us, then, whose hearts long to enter fully into communion with the Lord and God of all, stand with the myrrh-bearing women at the tomb of the heart and encounter there the mystery of death and new life. God stands with us, seeking our prayer even more ardently than the women sought the body of their Lord. Let His grace and love kindle within us the fervor to rise up to His calling! Let us attain true prayer through humility, obedience, and love, that we may stand before His throne on the great day of judgment with hearts transfigured by His mercy, to cry aloud with all creation: Glory to Thee Who hast given us life, Father, Son and Holy Spirit, now and ever, and to the ages of ages!

AMEN!

✠

---

[42] The Paschal greeting.

The creation, in Eden, of Eve from the rib of Adam by the Word of God, overshadowed by the Crucifixion of the Incarnate Word, *the Lamb slain before the foundation of the world* (Apoc. 13:8). Detail of a sixteenth-century Russian icon, now located in the Sol'vychegodsk Museum of History and Art, Russia.

A Postscript: Prayer and the Cross

THE BEGINNINGS of prayer have built within us a true desire to obtain the Kingdom, to dwell continuously in the embrace of God, to have our hearts illumined and warmed by the light of the Lord's presence. We have dwelt a little on what prayer is, what it can be, in our lives; but we cannot end without returning to the place where we began our discussion of prayer: the Cross of Christ, on which our Saviour is glorified, by which the world is transformed and creation renewed.

That which might be called prayer is not Christian prayer if it is not given shape by the Cross. We cannot know God, much less abide and rest in Him, unless we can say first and foremost with St. Paul, "I know only Christ, and Him crucified."[1] The Cross, and with it the Lord's glorious Resurrection, is the foundation of the universe, and so also the necessary foundation of our prayer. But what does this mean? What does it mean to see the crucified Lord of Glory at the center of every act in a life of prayer?

Let us first ask, what is there in the world that keeps the Christian from prayer? We cannot say that there is anything intrinsic to the world itself, anything "natural" or fundamental that works against our communion in God. The Lord Himself has fashioned this world—and indeed, all the cosmos—for the very purpose of our growing closer to Him and coming more fully into His divine embrace. The world has been forged by the Creator to be our support in prayer.

Nonetheless, the world does combat us, and any small step toward God reveals in a new way that we are *not of this world*.[2]

---

[1] Cf. I Corinthians 2:2.
[2] John 18:36. Cf. John 15:19, 17:15–18; Romans 12:2.

This is, let us state again, not because the world is evil or flawed, but because our sin has caused the gentle creation to become hostile. Through our transgression, the symphony of creation is upset and its song has become disorganized, jarring, and discordant. The heavens, which would show forth the glory of God,[3] instead seem to trap us in the earthbound immobility of our aimlessness. The sun and moon, which the Lord has fashioned to mark the hours of their setting[4] and give order to our growth into holiness, instead seem to present an endless cycle of futility and meaningless wandering. And all the societies that man has created over his long history, though born of God's merciful act in fashioning woman and giving our first forefather a companion, since *it is not good that man should be alone,*[5] nonetheless have come to enslave the mind, the heart, and the will into debased conceptions of freedom, of right, of morality—even of God.

So the world comes to combat the Life in Christ, not by its nature but by our mutilation of its nature. God has taken the dust and fashioned the clay, and at each measure beheld divinely that *it was very good;*[6] but we have taken that which is good and made of it a tool of mockery and death. Let us remember that the crown of thorns, by which the innocent Saviour was mocked and abused, was first the branch of a bush whose seed the same Son had fashioned, whose life was His doing; and the Cross on which we crucified the Lord of Glory was first a tree, whose rising up as a young sapling out of the tender earth was the creative work of the same Maker and Fashioner Who would die upon its beams. Would the measure of our sin not have intervened, we might have seen in these same fruits of the Lord's creation a new bush that would not be consumed by flame, we might have

---

[3] Cf. Psalm 18:1.
[4] Cf. Psalm 103:19.
[5] Genesis 2:18.
[6] Genesis 1:31.

watched there grow in Sion the Tree of Life watered by the dew of God.

Yet these became the instruments of death. So it is, too, with all creation: we have debased that which the Lord has fashioned for our glory, and now, standing in the midst of the earth, we say, "Who is there to help me, and where shall I find any relief?" We find foes that would hinder our prayer, our growth, our very life. We discover that we are not merely weak in prayer, but that we are opposed in prayer. The world opposes us, as the Lord said to His disciples: *If the world hates you, you know that it hated Me before it hated you.*[7]

But in this great disaster, in this catastrophe of our sin, we must not lose heart, for the mercy of God is greater than the feeble perception of our sinful eyes and our broken sense of history. We must not grow weary or weak. Rather, we must see in this very mystery the signs of God's glory and power. How weak, how weak are our eyes, when we see the bush become a crown and a tree become a Cross, and think that the fire of God is weakened or the Tree of Life lost. Far from it! Behold, the Cross is mystically the Tree itself.[8] Despite our sin—indeed, in a most wonderful and mystical way, even *through* our sin—the Lord has revealed the full measure of His glory. The Tree of Life escaped man's grasp in Eden, when his transgression with the fruit barred the way to it; but at Golgotha that very Tree, whose truest fruit is the self-sacrificing Saviour, stood in the midst of man's sin, at its very heart, and embraced the fallen, apostate, and rebellious of every generation. And while in Eden Adam and Eve could no longer

---

[7] John 15:18.

[8] In her hymns, the Church likens the Cross to the Tree of Life in Eden: "O wondrous miracle! Today, the Cross is beheld raised above the earth as a Jerusalem oak teeming with life, which held the Most High. By the Cross, we have all been drawn to God, and death is swallowed up. O undefiled Tree! Through you we delight in the immortal food in Eden, glorifying Christ" (Praises at Matins at the Sunday after the Elevation of the Precious Cross).

eat from the fruit of that Tree once they had broken communion with their Lord, today every true Christian may eat of the Tree of Life freely, each time he approaches the chalice and receives the Body and Blood of the Son.

This is how God transforms the weight of the world's sin into the glory of our redemption—and for this reason, we must not lose heart when we see the ways in which the world works to combat our prayer. The very things by which it seeks to crush us may become the means of our salvation; and the very resources by which it seeks to quash our prayer may become those by which our prayer blossoms. We may be tempted, tired, hunted, mocked, discouraged; but in the broken heart the Lord of Glory is enthroned. When the world is at its most ferocious in keeping us from the depth of the Life in Christ, when its attacks are in full force, we must remember that at these precise moments the words of the Lord are our guideposts: *Rejoice then, and be exceeding glad—for great is your reward in heaven.*[9]

Great indeed is the reward of those who will allow the crucifixion of their heart in order to welcome within it the crucified Son of God. Their reward is great, not because of any power or right or merit, but because the Christian's power is made perfect in weakness,[10] and that power is God Himself. It is the Cross that is the throne of the Lord's glory—the "throne of the Glory of His Kingdom," as it is called in the Divine Liturgy.[11] So, then, it is in the Cross that we, too, will find our resurrection. There we will find our prayer. There we will find our salvation.

To God be the glory, forever!

---

[9] Matthew 5:12.

[10] Cf. II Corinthians 12:9.

[11] From the prayers of the priest as he approaches the High Place during the singing of the Trisagion hymn.

Resurrectional icon of Christ descending into hades, bearing the Cross as a sign of victory. Russian icon of the fourteenth century, now located in the Walters Art Gallery, Baltimore.

Scriptural Index

The following Scriptural passages are either quoted directly or clearly referred to in the texts that make up this volume. All Old Testament references are to the book ordering and versification of the Septuagint (LXX).

Genesis

1:31 122
2:7 . . . . 62, 91, 105
2:18 122
2–3 66
3:1–4 34
3:5 47
11:1–9 86
32:30 69

Exodus

14 85
20:12 112
33:11 69

Leviticus

19:18 112

Deuteronomy

5:16 112
15:9 . . . . 13, 55

Joshua

1:9 51

II Kingdoms

22:36 79

I Paraleipomenon (I Chronicles)

21:1 30

Psalms

4:4 . . . . 38n31
18:1 122
23:7 74
23:8 115
24:17, 18 14
37:5 101
38:10 79
45:11 73
65:10 15
103:19 122
118:126 . . . . 6n7
120:2 78

Prayer of Manasseh

v. 10 . . . . 14, 82

Proverbs
6:5 13
12:25 115

Wisdom
2:24 31

Sirach
9:13 13

Jonah
2:6 82

Malachi
3:2 15

Isaiah
43:1 61
48:10 15
53:7 . . . . 79, 100

Jeremiah
1:5 105

Ezekiel
37:1–14 84

Matthew
4:1–11 31
4:9 34
5:5 107
5:12 124
5:13 54
6:1–6 96

6:6 96
6:24 76
6:32 25
6:33 23
7:1 108
7:13 . . . . 60, 114
8:22 21
11:12 . . . . 14, 65
11:28 73
11:29 . . . . 73, 79
11:30 80
12:43–45 30
13:1–23 59
13:31–32 92
14:13–21 85
14:28–33 115
15:4 112
15:32–38 85
17:20 94
17:21 31
19:21 60
19:26 62
22:1–14 102
22:39 112
25:13 87
26:39 49
27:14 100
28:20 . . . . 14, 105

Mark
1:12–13 31
3:22–29 14
4:35–41 101
5:36 101

5:41–42 68
6:30–44 85
7:10, 19 112
9:24 86
9:50 54
10:21 60
10:27 62
15:5 100

Luke

1:53 107
4:1–13 31
4:6 34
9:10–17 85
9:60 21
10:18 30
12:32 115
12:53 21
13:24 60
14:34 54
15:7 61
15:18–20 89
16:13 76
18:11 105
18:13 91
18:20 112
18:27 . . . . 14, 62
19:9 68
22:42 . . . . .49, 79
23:24 116
23:43 93

John

1:9 66

2:1–11 85
4:14 54
5:8 61
6:1–14 85
6:38 79
8:2–11 99
8:44 . . . . 30, 32, 77
9:4 114
11:1–44 68
15:18 123
15:19 121
17:15–18 121
17:20, 21 . . . . .60n2
18:36 121
18:38 100
20:28 68

Acts

8:32 . . . . .79, 100

Romans

6:6 25
6:8 117
7:15 86
7:24 20
8:11 84
8:26 84
8:39 65
12:2 121

I Corinthians

2:2 121
2:7–10 66
3:16 96

13:1–8 94
13:13 92

II Corinthians
7:10 . . . . 39n33
12:9 124

Galatians
4:4 105
5:13 112

Ephesians
2:2 33
4:22 25
6:12 . . . . 31, 33

Philippians
2:5–11 46
2:8 79
2:9–10 . . . . 82, 109
4:8 113
4:13 14

Colossians
3:9 25

I Timothy
1:15 53

Hebrews
6:7 88
11:1 92
11:8, 9, 23–29 92

I Peter
1:18–20 66

I John
1:8 81
3:8 29
4:8, 16 94
4:18 115

Apocalypse
3:15, 16 54
13:8 . . . . 66, 120

SAINT HERMAN
OF ALASKA
BROTHERHOOD

Since 1965, the St. Herman of Alaska Brotherhood has been
publishing Orthodox Christian books and magazines.

View our catalog, featuring over fifty titles,
and order online, at
www.sainthermanmonastery.com

You can also write us for a free printout of our catalog:

St. Herman of Alaska Brotherhood
P. O. Box 70
Platina, CA 96076
U.S.A.